HOW TO MAKE

THE

BEST

COFFEE

AT HOME

HOW TO MAKE
THE
BEST
COFFEE
AT HOME

JAMES HOFFMANN

MITCHELL BEAZLEY

For Beth, Lyla and Theo.

First published in Great Britain in 2022 by Mitchell Beazley, an imprint of Octopus
Publishing Group Ltd, Carmelite House, 50 Victoria Embankment, London, EC4Y 0DZ
www.octopusbooks.co.uk

An Hachette UK Company
www.hachette.co.uk

Distributed in the US by Hachette Book Group, 1290 Avenue of the Americas, 4th and
5th Floors, New York, NY 10104

Distributed in Canada by Canadian Manda Group, 664 Annette St., Toronto, Ontario,
Canada M6S 2C8

ISBN 978-1-78472-724-6

A CIP catalogue record for this book is available from the British Library.

Printed and bound in China

10 9 8 7 6 5

Group Publisher: Denise Bates
Senior Editor: Pollyanna Poulter
Art Director: Juliette Norsworthy
Designers: Leonardo Collina, Lizzie Ballantyne
Special photography: Cristian Barnett
Illustrator: Claire Huntley
Picture research: Giulia Hetherington and Jennifer Veall
Senior Production Controller: Allison Gonsalves

This FSC® label means that materials used for the product have been responsibly sourced.

CONTENTS

INTRODUCTION

A cup of coffee can be many things: a jolt of caffeine, fuel for our work, a social lubricant, a necessity or a luxury. It can be surprising, delightful and delicious, and it can transport you around the world. It can also be a lot of fun.

Coffee is produced in dozens of countries around the world, is consumed in every single country and has wrapped itself up in many different cultures in many different ways. Drinking the roasted, pulverized and infused seeds of the fruit from a small tropical shrub is a very human act.

Coffee, especially the modern speciality coffee movement in the last decade or two, has gained a reputation as being a bit serious, too earnest, occasionally pretentious and something requiring study and education in order to enjoy. As I start this book, a book full of the intricacies and minutiae of great coffee, I think it is important for both you and I to remember that the goal is fun, that the goal is enjoyment above all else.

I want to share the things that have helped me make better coffee, while also highlighting what makes it surprising, delightful and intriguing. It doesn't have to be those things every day, it can just be a gentle and welcome liquid light-switch for your brain in the morning – because some mornings that's all we really want it to be.

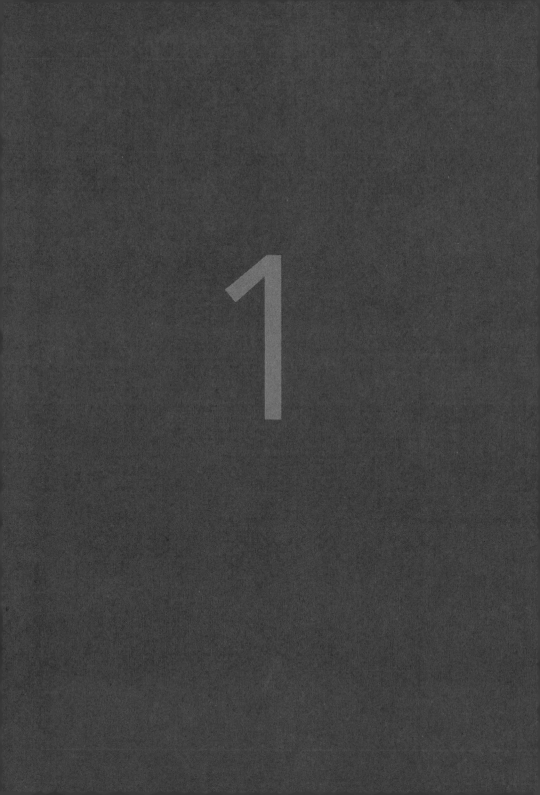

1

HOW TO BUY GREAT COFFEE

You'll hear over and over again that a great cup of coffee can't exist without great raw materials. All the technique and equipment in the world can't overcome the limitations of the coffee you are brewing. However, there is no real arbiter of what is 'good'. There are definitions of speciality coffee that exist, but that doesn't mean that people should aspire to all like the same kinds of coffee. The joy of coffee, once you dig into it, is the diversity of flavour.

The speciality coffee industry ran into a bit of a wall in its early years by telling people that they should drink 'better' coffee. People, quite rightly, didn't like the inference that what they had been buying, drinking and *enjoying just fine thank you very much* was inferior.

Yet here I am, about to make a similar case but with some caveats. I would argue that whatever you enjoy right now, there's probably something out there that you'd enjoy even more and that a little exploration will be incredibly rewarding – and, frankly, surprisingly fun. This chapter aims to break apart the process of buying coffee so that you can explore risk free. I don't like the idea of someone trying something different to their usual choice and hating it. I think this can be avoided, and we can also remove a few of the myths and misconceptions that exist around the coffee-buying experience.

Freshness

One of the great successes of coffee's marketing has been the idea that 'fresher is better'.

You see 'fresh ground coffee' or 'freshly brewed coffee' everywhere, and actually shifting the mindset for many people so that they see coffee as fresh produce, not a shelf-stable staple, is good news. Coffee degrades relatively slowly compared to other fresh produce, and you could argue that because it is safe to drink at a couple of years old, then it really is a shelf-stable product. If you want the best value for money, then drinking your coffee while fresh is a real win. Before I talk about how long coffee lasts, I should briefly discuss the ways in which coffee goes stale.

Loss of volatiles: By volatiles, I'm talking about volatile aromatic compounds, the compounds assessed and enjoyed by your olfactory bulb, experienced as aroma or flavour. As coffee ages, a significant quantity of its flavours literally escape the beans or the grounds, often into the atmosphere. This is possible to slow with better packaging but you'll always lose nuance, flavour and delight over time.

Development of new/bad flavours: The compounds in coffee that you taste and enjoy are, sadly, not inert. Over time they react with each other and begin to form new compounds. Not always, but often, these are less enjoyable than the ones you started with.

Rancidification: Coffee contains lipids in the form of fats or oils, and these are susceptible to turning rancid. It might be oxygen causing oxidation or it might be moisture leading to the breakdown of the fats. Either way, this pretty quickly causes some unpleasant and undesirable flavours to appear. Darker roasts have more of the oils pushed to the surface of the coffee bean, meaning they're more likely to interact with any air or moisture present, so these develop rancid flavours more quickly.

I'm going to add one more here, even though this doesn't strongly correlate to negative flavours, because it is worth understanding before continuing the discussion of freshness.

Degassing: During the coffee-roasting process, a host of chemical reactions are going on which result in the coffee turning brown and a lot of the flavours we love being created. A by-product of all this is carbon dioxide (CO_2). A lot of it, if we're talking volume. One kilogramme of coffee produces about 10 litres of carbon dioxide in the roasting process. Most of this escapes during the roast, and what is retained in the coffee bean at the end of the roast still does a pretty good job of escaping in the first few hours after roasting.

from the grounds. If a lot of CO_2 is coming out of the grounds, then it is harder for the water to extract the coffee. A frustrating truth of coffee (and there are several in this book) is that the staler coffee gets, the easier it is to brew and extract. Though, of course, the staler the coffee gets, the worse your resulting cup will taste.

The shift to e-commerce in coffee has set the expectation that a coffee company roasts and ships to order. Coupled with wider e-commerce shortening delivery time expectations, this means that most coffee bought online arrives too fresh. For the best experience, you should wait – often termed 'resting' the coffee. How long should you wait? How long is the window of goodness before the stale flavours kick in?

Coffee Beans and Freshness

Keeping coffee beans whole dramatically increases their lifespan. There are no hard rules here, and it is also worth bearing in mind that storage conditions can play a big role, especially temperature. Higher ambient temperatures will cause coffee to turn stale faster, as the heat supplies lots of energy to accelerate the staling process.

Compared to what you started with, relatively little is retained by the beans by the time they're packaged but, and this is an important but, there's still enough to have a significant impact on the way that the coffee brews.

For this reason, coffee can be 'too fresh', especially if you plan to use it in an espresso machine. When you brew coffee, water coming into contact with the ground coffee seems to liberate a lot of the trapped CO_2. In the brewing section (see pages 87–129) you'll often see a reference to 'blooming' where a little water is added to the coffee before the bulk of the brewing happens, to help extract the CO_2

If you're brewing coffee as espresso, I would recommend waiting at least 7–8 days after roasting before starting to brew the coffee. Once you open a bag, if you store it properly, then you'll continue to have great results over the next couple of weeks. After that you'll begin to notice a real drop in how good the coffee tastes. Over the 2 weeks of use you'll see a steady drop in the amount of crema the coffee produces because that crema is just trapped CO_2 (for more on crema and what it is, see page 154). However, that doesn't mean the coffee will taste bad.

If you're brewing it as filter coffee, then you can get good results 4–5 days after roasting. You won't see as big an impact from its freshness on its ability to be brewed and extracted properly even 2 or 3 days off roast, compared with espresso. Similarly to espresso, once you open the bag, then you've got a couple of weeks where you'll get the best-tasting coffee, and a steady decline from that point onward.

Ideal Coffee Freshness – Ground Coffee

Once you grind coffee, the staling reactions begin to pick up the pace very quickly. In a side-by-side testing, many people would spot a clear difference between 12-hours-old and fresh coffee, and most people would spot the difference between 24-hours-old and fresh. How much that difference bothers them is hard to predict, but it is clear. By the time the coffee is 48 hours old I think I'd struggle to find someone who didn't consider it to taste worse.

I advocate grinding coffee for the following different reasons:

- it smells amazing, and will make your morning/day more delightful every time you do it.

- buying whole-bean coffee is better value. Pre-ground coffee can cost the same but overall makes comparatively worse-tasting coffee, so is worse value.

- grinding yourself means you can get the best from the coffee – by adjusting the grind size depending on the variety, the brewer and your personal preferences.

I accept that the downsides of grinding your own coffee are that there's some inconvenience compared with just grabbing a bag of grounds, and that there's also the cost of buying a coffee grinder to factor in. But I think a coffee grinder is an incredibly valuable investment in your kitchen set-up and I'll go deeper into coffee grinders later (see pages 54–60).

Storing Coffee

The best way to store coffee for daily use is in something dark, dry and airtight.

Many bags now come with resealable strips and they're as good as anything else I've tested. There are lots of coffee canisters available for sale, and while I think vacuum storage ones have a very slight edge, you should just pick something that you like the look and price of which closes airtight.

I'd avoid putting coffee in the refrigerator. In theory it should be better than a cupboard because it is cooler, and as long as it is stored airtight then that would be true. However, bringing coffee in and out of the refrigerator can result in accelerated staling caused by condensation forming on the cold coffee. Also, if the bag is open, the coffee can easily pick up flavours from anything particularly aromatic in your refrigerator.

The freezer is an excellent place to store coffee long term. Coffee, sealed airtight and ideally with as little air as possible in the package, will last months in a freezer. Taking the coffee in and out of the freezer is bad because of condensation, but some people like to store single doses in their freezer and pull out only what they need for that day's cup. This works well, though does involve a significant amount of labour and packing prep when you are storing a new bag of coffee.

Where You Buy Coffee

Where you buy your coffee will have a significant impact on its freshness and age.

I'll cover the three main places people tend to buy coffee, and the impacts of each one:

The Supermarket/Grocery Store

Historically this is where most people bought their coffee, and that has only really started to change in the last decade. Supermarkets treat coffee like a shelf-stable product. Coffee doesn't have a 'Use by' date, it has a 'Best before' date because even after a couple of years it is likely to be safe to consume, though inarguably past its best. Large companies do not put roast dates on their products – because supermarkets don't want them to. Supermarket supply chains mean that coffee can be weeks or months old before it hits store shelves. It hits the back of those shelves, and then it slowly works its way forward.

If you pick up a bag that has 7 months left before the best before date, that also feels more like good news than picking up a bag and finding out that it is 5 months old. In addition there's no standard for best before dates in coffee, so some companies will use 12 months, some 18 and others up to 24 months from roast. Some smaller, more quality-focused companies that have started working with supermarkets will often put a 'use by' on there as requested, but will also add a 'roasted on' date to the packaging – though rarely as obvious as the use by. It is hard to buy truly fresh coffee in most supermarkets. Some local shops and retailers may do a better job, but it is very much the luck of the draw at that point.

A Local Coffee Shop

This is an excellent place to buy coffee, not just because I believe in supporting local businesses. Coffee shops now regularly retail the coffee they are serving. This coffee is often quite nicely rested, maybe a week old when it is on the shelves, and that means that coffee shops are the perfect place to go if you need coffee to brew right now. As a bonus, you can have a conversation with someone about the coffee, and talk to them about your preferences, which means you're more likely to find something you'll enjoy than working your way through the labels in a supermarket (I'll talk more about labels on page 22). As a final bonus, you can often taste the coffee

before you buy – great for both reducing the risk you'll hate it and also giving you a bit of a benchmark for how the coffee tastes for you to chase in your home brewing.

Online

It is now easier than ever to buy great coffee online, and the explosion in the number of coffee roasters worldwide has definitely benefitted the consumer. The experience of buying online is often excellent, competitively priced and with quick delivery times. However, there's limited human interaction which, while often appealing, makes getting recommendations more difficult. Most coffee-roasting companies will explicitly state their policies on roasting and shipping. Smaller companies don't have the volume to roast every day, so may either hold your order until the next production day or send coffee a day or two old. As I've said, super-fresh coffee isn't necessarily the best for brewing, but online buying should at least provide a predictable flow of coffee, and hopefully you can order to have your coffee arrive up to a week before your current stocks run out.

Most coffee roasters offer subscription services, where coffee is sent out automatically each week, fortnight or month. There are a broad range of experiences from 'send me the thing I like every week, so I don't have to remember' through to 'send me something new and different every single time'.

PRICE

This should be the easiest and most obvious indicator of quality – the more it costs, the better it should be. That is, of course, impossible in a world with diverse preferences and definitions of 'good'. However, I still need to talk about price when it comes to buying coffee.

Having a bag of coffee at home is normal for hundreds of millions of households. It is, if you stop and think about it for a second, astonishing that it is possible. You have the seeds of a tropical plant, grown thousands of miles away, that have been harvested, processed, sorted, exported, roasted, packaged and delivered to your door for a very small cost. This sets the expectation early on that coffee should be cheap, and sadly some coffee will probably always be inexpensive. But cheap coffee comes at a very human cost – someone must struggle for your coffee to be low-priced; someone must live a life of food insecurity or inescapable debt. Cheap coffee is nothing to celebrate, now or ever.

It will come as no surprise that I think coffee is undervalued; it is a fascinating beverage that not only is delicious and diverse but also psychoactive and stimulating. It is something I encourage you to invest in if you can.

Paying a little extra for your morning brew and avoiding large, multinational brands that work to keep coffee prices low, is better for everyone involved. Paying a premium for top-end speciality coffees does not fix the injustice of the coffee industry, nor is it transformative for any individual farmer. However, paying sustainable prices for any and all coffee you buy is valuable and worthwhile. To give you an exact target figure will immediately date this book, but the baseline prices you see from speciality roasters are good ones to aim for.

I dislike the idea that spending more is my best current advice, especially as poverty and food insecurity are common in consuming countries as well as producing countries. But I cannot advocate keeping coffee cheap when we've seen the impact of this practice on the lives of millions of coffee-producing families around the world.

Roast Level

With the rise of speciality coffee in the last 20 years it does appear that coffee companies talking about the roast level of the coffee has become deeply unfashionable. There can be enormous amounts of information presented on the label, but roast level is rarely one of them.

There are probably a few reasons for this. Many smaller speciality coffee companies are working under the idea that they've found their ideal roast profile for this particular coffee, and they believe that no other roast level would be suitable. Secondly, speciality roasts are often in the spectrum of light to medium as the current style of roasting remains still something of a counter movement to the darker roasting styles of companies like Starbucks. Finally, and perhaps most frustratingly, there are no real standards out there for what constitutes a light, medium or dark roast. However, I still believe that this information would be helpful in making a decision for many coffee buyers. With speciality companies you are often best to presume that everything is light to medium in roast unless explicitly labelled otherwise.

Historically, coffee has been labelled by roast in a slightly obtuse way, through the use of a strength rating. The modern coffee industry has long argued that this practice is confusing, because strength comes primarily from the way that you brew the coffee and the ratio of coffee to water that you use. However, darker roasts are more soluble than lighter roasts, so if I'm nitpicking then strength labels are ironically pretty accurate.

What these labels are really communicating is the intensity of bitterness that you're likely to experience from a particular coffee. However, whether they use a 5- or 10-point scale, you tend to find that the range starts in the middle and goes up from there – because no one wants their coffee to have the lowest possible strength rating.

How Roasting Affects Flavour

How you roast a coffee has a dramatic effect on its taste. The longer you roast a coffee, the more you generate what are often described as generic roast flavours. These flavours generate in most products that you roast to brown, such as bread or chocolate. Eventually these turn into harsher, more burned-tasting flavours. This also correlates with an increase in bitterness, much as sugar gets more bitter the darker you take it as caramel. Alongside this increase in bitterness, you also generally see a decrease in acidity.

Acidity is a complex topic in coffee, and also pretty divisive. Acidity often correlates with the density of the coffee, which is about how it grew. Coffee grown at higher altitudes grows more slowly and is denser. It often has more aromatic complexity and a greater capacity for sweetness – though this isn't linear, so don't just look for the highest grown coffee you can find. Interesting, complex and flavourful coffees tend to have higher levels of acidity.

For a coffee roaster, the challenge is to keep as much of the inherent character of the coffee, building a supporting layer of pleasing roasted flavours and balancing out the acidity in the coffee to make it a pleasurable experience all around. Acidity adds contrast, juiciness, crispness, excitement and can be delightful. It can also be sour, harsh and miserably unpleasant if the roast is executed badly.

Roasting coffee isn't just difficult because finding this moment of balance between sweet, acidic and bitter requires precision and a lot of practical experience. It is also difficult because we don't all agree exactly where that point is. This makes roasting part practical food manufacture and part philosophical or aesthetic. A company often has a collective idea of how great coffee should taste, with the understanding that not everyone who drinks coffee will agree with them.

This is why there's no real agreement on what a medium roast is. Everyone is starting from slightly different points on the roast colour spectrum. As an extreme example, Starbucks' lightest roast (their Blonde Roast) is darker than anything most speciality companies will ever roast.

Traceability

For a long time I used traceability as the best shortcut for buying excellent coffee. If a coffee came from a very specific place, a farm, a cooperative or specific mill, then it was likely to be pretty good quality.

The process of keeping a lot of coffee separate throughout the supply chain, from farm to cup, adds cost. This investment is only worth it if the coffee can be sold for a premium based on its flavour, i.e. if the coffee is high quality. This isn't a perfect shortcut, but it is a pretty effective one.

What is challenging to someone looking at a row of different bags of coffee is understanding which ones are properly traceable and which ones just look it on the surface. You can't just recommend people only buy coffee from single estates because of the complexities of land ownership. In many coffee-producing countries you would be excluding many great producers (and coffees) because they don't own enough land to be considered a farm. In Kenya you might buy amazing coffee that came from a single washing station, which processed coffee for hundreds, if not thousands, of producers. That could be some of the best coffee from Kenya, but that same level of traceability in Costa Rica wouldn't get you to the best coffee. In an effort to offer better guidance I ended up writing *The World Atlas of Coffee* to try and break this information down in detail, country by country. But I'd still advocate traceability as the most useful indicator of quality.

Post-harvest Process

On a typical bag of speciality coffee there's often a lot of information about the coffee itself. That information will vary in scope and detail from roaster to roaster, but one of the pieces I think is particularly important – and thankfully pretty much always present – is the post-harvest process used.

When you pick coffee fruit, you're aiming to do so at peak ripeness, despite the fact that it isn't the fruit you want but the seeds inside. How you get the seeds from the fruit has a big impact on their flavour. This isn't the place to go into detail about that process; instead I want to focus on the impact on flavour and one particular quality of flavour in coffee: ferment.

Historically, fermented flavours were not considered desirable in many coffees, and processes were created to minimize those qualities. The washed process, where you squeeze the seeds out of the fruit, run a small fermentation to break down any fruit flesh that is stuck to the seed, and then wash it clean before drying, was focused on minimizing fermented or 'off' flavours by getting rid of the sugar in the fruit flesh as quickly as possible to prevent that sugar fuelling questionable flavour development.

The challenge of the washed, or wet, process is the amount of water needed. The least water-intensive process is the natural, or dry, method. Here you dry the whole cherry straight after picking and later hull it to get at the seeds inside. Drying whole fruit in the sun can lead to some uncontrolled chemistry, which produces fermented fruit flavours. Some people love these flavours – they love blueberry, mango, pineapple or other tropical notes in their coffee. Other people find these flavours repugnant – to them they are closer to rotten fruit than to a fun fruit salad. Finding out how you feel about fermented flavours in coffee is a really helpful piece of guidance for future coffee buying.

There's no morally superior answer here; it is OK to like or dislike whatever you do. The coffee industry itself is split – some roasters won't buy and roast naturally processed coffees. They believe that the process smothers the inherent taste of the terroir with the flavour of processing. I think it is important that roasters have a vision and believe in the products they sell, so I support both sides here and both have audiences for their approach.

Other processes tend to leave more fruit flesh on the coffee – such as the honey process or pulped natural process. It is difficult to make sweeping statements about how

these processes affect taste because they're employed in a variety of ways. In addition, there are increasing numbers of boutique and experimental fermentations going on with washed coffees. These processes are usually labelled clearly, often with flamboyant language, so you are unlikely to mistake them for normal washed coffees.

Bourbon

Catuai

Kona

Gesha

Variety

Wine has done a great job of communicating the impact of variety on taste. Most wine drinkers have opinions on a glass of Chardonnay or Cabernet Sauvignon.

Coffee is often sold by variety too, though I would rarely recommend buying based on trying one coffee variety once and looking for it again. Coffee varieties are chosen by producers often for very practical reasons. Some varieties have higher yields, some varieties grow as shorter trees, which makes them easier to pick by hand. Many producers have limited access to seed stocks, so they are choosing from limited choices.

Some coffee varieties do have flavour characteristics that manifest regardless of terroir, but these are relatively rare. I think it is very, very difficult to drink a cup of coffee and know if the coffee is bourbon variety or caturra variety.

Roasters will often list the variety of the coffee on the label of the bag, but this is often more valuable as a demonstration of traceability than it is as guidance for enjoyment.

Rarely do roasters contextualize a variety either – you need to be quite deeply into coffee to know that seeing Wush Wush grown in Colombia is quite rare, or that bourbon coffee grown in Indonesia is unusual.

Varieties like Gesha (often embarrassingly styled as Geisha), do have consistent floral and citrus flavours that make them unusual as well as relatively valuable. However, I'd say 90 per cent of the varieties you see would be difficult to write descriptors for.

What Flavour Notes Mean

Flavour notes in coffee are both a standardized norm and somewhat contentious and controversial.

What I want to cover here is how to read them to pick apart key attributes of the coffee-drinking experience, in the hope of making choosing one bag out of a dozen or more easier, and more likely to result in you being delighted by your decision.

I believe there are three key attributes of coffee drinking that drive a love/loathe experience for most people:

Acidity: As we have seen on page 24, acidity is a complex topic. Some people love acidity in coffee, and some people find it misplaced and unpleasant. I'd argue some acidity is part of what makes speciality coffee special, but balance is everything.

Fruity flavours: As I covered on pages 28–9, at one end of the spectrum are the fermented fruit flavours. A significant percentage of coffee drinkers hate these flavours, while a similar-sized audience absolutely adore them, with the majority open to them. At the other end of the spectrum, you'll find coffee with no fruit qualities and in the middle you'll have what I'd describe as clean fruit flavours.

Texture: How a coffee feels to drink is important, but considering its value to people it is rarely discussed. Coffee can be light, almost tea-like, it can be heavy and rich, and it can be everything in between.

Decoding Packaging Descriptors

The words used on a bag of coffee can be interpreted to give you some ideas of how the coffee will fit within the above categories. It isn't absolute, and nothing is going to replace a conversation with someone who has tasted everything that they're selling, but I think it is useful.

Fresh fruit flavours: If you see berry fruits, pome fruits (apples, pears etc.) or citrus fruits on a label, then I would expect relatively high acidity. These coffees will likely be quite sweet, but if you hate acidity then I'd be hesitant if these flavours take up the bulk or are the primary descriptors. These coffees will often be light to medium bodied.

Tropical fruit flavours: I'd include strawberry and blueberry in this list too, but mango, lychee, pineapple and others would likely indicate fermented flavours in the coffee, and if you don't enjoy them, then I'd avoid that particular bag. These kinds of coffees tend to be a little heavier bodied.

Cooked fruit flavours: If you see any references to cooked or processed fruit, such as jams, jellies or pie (i.e. cherry pie), then these coffees tend to have some acidity but it isn't as dominant. These coffees are often a little more full-bodied than the more acidic counterparts.

Browning flavours: I wish there were a better descriptor, but there is a wide category of flavours that come from the browning reactions during roasting. You'll often see chocolate, nuts, caramel, toffee and others on labels. If you see this with an absence of fruit, then I'd expect comparatively low acidity and often these coffees are medium- to full-bodied.

Bitter flavours: For dark roasts you may see smokier flavours, dark chocolate or sometimes things like molasses listed. Expect heavy body, limited to no acidity but more bitterness front and centre.

It would be fair to accuse me of being reductive here. The delight of great coffee is its diversity; there is a staggering and surprising variety of experiences possible in a single cup and I don't want people to miss out on that. I encourage you to test the boundaries of your own preferences, but the above guidance is there to help you avoid buying a bag that you're angry to have to finish because deep down you want to throw it away and never drink it again.

Finally, this is a time of great competition and many roasters are keen to try and build a relationship. If you buy a bag of coffee and you hate it, then let them know – almost all would love the opportunity to offer you something you'd really like and to understand why their product disappointed you. They may not offer a coffee you love, but they'd rather understand that and you understand that than sell you a second disappointment.

2

THE ESSENTIALS FOR
GREAT COFFEE

When you fall in love with coffee, it is hard to resist the temptation to begin acquiring and hoarding the paraphernalia that comes with it and upgrading your equipment. This can be a pleasurable part of any hobby, but it can also create a perceived barrier of entry for a beginner. In this section I want to cover the things that I think are absolutely essential, aside from your coffee brewer of choice.

With equipment I'll try to help you avoid the traps set by manufacturers offering extremely cheap options. These are often so compromised in their performance in order to meet price points they should be avoided completely. They are more hindrance than help, and investing in your coffee set-up should make the process more enjoyable as well as the cup more delicious. These kinds of machine will actively work against you, soon be rejected and become a burden of waste on your home and the environment.

It often feels like a fork in the road is presented to new coffee drinkers: do you want to proceed down the path of brewed coffee, or do you have plans to begin the steep climb up toward great espresso? It isn't quite as binary as that, but I will say that the path to great filter coffee is likely to be easier, less frustrating and cheaper too. I will do my best to give you the guidance you need to avoid the pitfalls and dead ends that crop up along each path.

The Best Water for Brewing Coffee

Discussing water for coffee brewing quickly becomes an emotive conversation because it is one of the most frustrating aspects as you begin to dig deeper into understanding why a cup of coffee might be good, or unexpectedly bad.

Water has two roles in coffee brewing: it is an ingredient and it is a solvent heavily involved in determining which flavours are dissolved when you brew. Dealing with it as an ingredient is far easier, as it makes up the vast majority of a cup of coffee. A cup of black filter coffee is around 98.5 per cent water and a typical espresso is still 90 per cent water. From this perspective, your main concern is that the water is clean and neutral-tasting, free of any taints like chlorine.

While many people reading this book will have good-tasting water straight from the tap, and I'll focus on getting the best from that when brewing coffee, I do want to cover fixing 'off' tastes. The most effective solution is to use an active carbon filter. These are cheap, and often a component of water filtration jugs, which also have a softening component. If softening isn't an issue, then you can usually find taste and odour filters that are just active carbon alongside a fine mesh designed to catch particles in your water too. These have a pretty long lifespan, though as with any water filter you have to be mindful of the potential for bacterial growth and change them often.

I'm going to look at all the factors that affect water for your coffee. I'm about to dive deeper into water chemistry and that can be off-putting for many people, again an area in which coffee can suddenly seem inaccessible, difficult and overly complicated. The goal here is not to turn your kitchen into a science lab (unless you want to), but to give you an understanding of what matters with water for coffee and how you might make the best choice for your preferences, budget and interest in coffee brewing.

Hard and Soft

When I talk about 'hard' water, I mean water that contains a substantial quantity of dissolved minerals like calcium and magnesium, picked up as the water has made its way through the ground. 'Soft' water conversely is low in these minerals.

I often talk about softening water to reduce its calcium carbonate content. This comes from dissolved limestone, and when it precipitates out of hot liquid it forms the limescale you see in your kettle or your coffee machine. You need relatively soft water to produce good-tasting coffee but that's not all.

I'll say at the start that if you're using clean-tasting, relatively soft water, then you're most of the way there. However, I will state right now that distilled or pure water is a bad choice for coffee brewing. It makes bad-tasting coffee, and is actually corrosive inside a coffee machine or kettle, so is best avoided.

If you're unsure if your water is hard or soft, take a look inside your kettle or anything that heats water. If you see limescale building up, then you've got hard water.

Minerals

Pick up a bottle of mineral water in most parts of the world, and you'll see a list of the minerals it contains on the side. When it comes to dissolved minerals and coffee, there are two in particular that we are interested in: calcium and magnesium. Both get directly involved in coffee brewing, helping extract the delicious soluble compounds in ground coffee into your brewing water. Water without these minerals won't do as good a job as water with some. The more of these minerals you have, the more you will extract, but that doesn't mean that more is always better.

Extracting more from coffee can result in an unbalanced, acidic and overwhelming cup. This is also a point at which calcium and magnesium act differently. Water with a higher magnesium content is often more acidic, with a different flavour profile, compared to calcium. High magnesium levels aren't particularly common in tap water, certainly compared to high calcium levels, and magnesium doesn't form limescale either.

High calcium levels are common in many parts of the world, and one of the ways many water filters work is to exchange calcium for a different ion, often sodium coming from water filters that use table salt. (Because only sodium is substituted, rather than sodium chloride, these filters don't make the water taste salty.) There are other ion-exchange water filters that can affect water for coffee, specifically its alkalinity, which I'll discuss opposite.

Finding an ideal level for calcium and magnesium is difficult because of the complicating factor of how limescale forms in hot water, comes out of solution and builds up inside equipment. The build-up of scale is a big concern in coffee equipment. While a kettle is easily descaled, an espresso or coffee machine is more complicated and time-consuming. Moreover, while you can easily see how scaled-up a kettle is when you open the lid to add water, it is not so easy to open coffee machines to see the state of scale build-up, so often the time you know you have an issue is when the equipment breaks.

The best-tasting water for coffee brewing may not be the best for preventing limescale build-up. So you're looking for a Goldilocks

that they act in a manner that regulates the pH of the water, or that of your coffee. While the pH of a beverage doesn't correlate exactly to how acidic it tastes, the buffer definitely has an impact on acidity in coffee.

Water has quite dramatically different levels of alkalinity, and this has a direct and surprising impact on coffee. Too little alkalinity and the coffee can taste sour and harsh. Too much, and the coffee becomes muted and flat. Once again it feels like you're chasing another Goldilocks zone but (while there are options on the market for water filters that address alkalinity as well as hardness) it is more about understanding why your coffee at home may taste a certain way. Ideally alkalinity would correlate in a fixed way with the water's minerals. More mineral content means more extraction, and more alkalinity prevents the higher extraction from being unpleasantly sour or acidic. However, the real world rarely works that way.

Recommended Water Ranges

This is important: there is no singular 'best' water recipe. People have different preferences and expectations for their coffee, and water can and should play a role in that. Not everyone wants high extraction with crisp, bright acidity. Not everyone drinks the same style of coffee, and what some people want from different roast levels might mean that they get great results with their tap water

zone where coffee tastes good and you're not at risk of damaging your coffee machine. Thankfully there's a pretty wide window there, and the point of this chapter is to help you make informed decisions, rather than to create anxiety about something that should be uncomplicated: the water from your taps.

Alkalinity

Minerals are half the story when it comes to how your water interacts with coffee. When calcium carbonate (limestone) is dissolved from the bedrock, as part of its long journey from a raincloud to your tap, it is present there in its ions: calcium and bicarbonate. Bicarbonate ions act as a buffer. The simplest explanation is

answers to every question on this subject. That said, there are a few ways to get the best water for your coffee brewing.

Start with Your Tap Water

The first thing to do is to understand the mineral content of your tap water. In many parts of the world this information is available online from water suppliers, usually with postcode or ZIP code accuracy. If that isn't an option, then you can pick up a water test kit very cheaply online. The best value kits are those targeting home aquarium owners, who will know the pain of maintaining ideal water conditions all too well. These kits should last a long time should you feel the need to retest – which is particularly useful for those homes that have a variation in the source of their water supply throughout the year.

while a neighbour may be a touch frustrated with the same water with a different roast.

Water recipe guidance is often presented in a chart, as opposite, with hardness (your total mineral content) along the y-axis and alkalinity on the x-axis. I would recommend a fairly broad range, with the caveat that if you're trying to squeeze the last drops of excellence from your coffee, then you may look to your water recipe as an opportunity for tweaking and incremental improvement.

How to Get Great Water for Coffee

All of the previous theory has to manifest into something practical, though I'll be upfront and say that we don't have satisfying

If your water isn't far outside the recommended range (see opposite), then I'd suggest using a simple water filter jug. The units from Brita or BWT are widely available, and the Peak Water jugs are a more coffee-focused option (as they test alkalinity). These are relatively cheap, convenient and the ion exchange inside the filters can be re-used and recycled very efficiently if you return them. (Most offer a postage-paid solution for this.) The only thing to note is that these kinds of water filters can be susceptible to mould and bacterial growth so you should change it every month, regardless of how

RECOMMENDED WATER RANGES – CHART

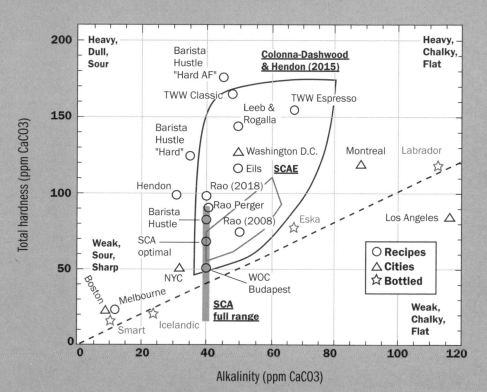

There's no single best recipe or water, but you'll generally find a balance between the hardness and the alkalinity in either recommended recipes you can find online, bottled waters or the tap water of certain cities.

The above chart was created by Jonathan Gagné, author of *The Physics of Filter Coffee* (2021). Ultimately, it highlights various studies done on water chemistry and coffee brewing (by the Specialty Coffee Association of America, SCAA, and the Specialty Coffee Association of Europe, SCAE) as well as a range published by Maxwell Colonna-Dashwood and Christopher Hendon in their book *Water for Coffee* (2015). Essentially, any water that might find itself charting in the green, blue and red areas should brew well.

Water hardness levels are dictated by the parts per million (ppm) of minerals, including calcium carbonate ($CaCO_3$), in the water. Soft water typically has less than 50ppm of calcium carbonate and hard water has over 200ppm.

much you might have used it, as per the manufacturer's instructions.

If your water is a long way from where you want it to be, then you have a more extreme solution: strip everything from the water and remineralize it. The simplest way to do this would be to use a water filter like the Zero Water jug. This takes everything out, producing nearly pure water. You can then add minerals to it, either your own recipe (I'll touch on this opposite) or a product like Third Wave Water, a sachet of minerals which dissolves into distilled water to give great coffee-brewing water. This isn't excessively expensive, but it is more work.

The other option is to use something like a reverse osmosis (RO) filter. This is a machine that pushes water against a membrane filter so fine that only water can pass through and dissolved ions cannot. These are often used commercially in very hard water areas, but they have some significant downsides: they're expensive and they're wasteful. Generally an RO filter will take at least 2 litres of tap water in to produce 1 litre of filtered water. The other litre becomes waste, with a higher concentration of minerals. In some units you can use a small amount of this very hard water to blend back in to get your desired level of minerals, but for the home I'm not sure I can make that recommendation unless you have the budget and a need for a lot of soft water.

Recipe Water

At what seems like the extreme of water for coffee, you have homemade recipes for water. You can, with a little bit of effort at the start, cheaply and easily create custom water to your preferences or to other recommended recipes you might find online. I will reiterate now, for those who might find they have an extremely raised eyebrow, that water's impact on coffee is huge and for some people their tap water is too far away from ideal for any other solution to feel practical.

To make recipe water you need two components: minerals and alkalinity. You can use easily available sources of each, plus water and a set of scales:

Epsom salts: This is magnesium sulphate and an easy way to add magnesium to water.

Bicarbonate of soda (baking soda): This is sodium bicarbonate, which will add your buffer/alkalinity.

Distilled water: This can be filtered to pure in a Zero Water filter, or purchased as distilled or deionized water.

Scales accurate to 0.01g: These are available online and while the cheaper sets may not be truly accurate to 0.01g, they'll probably get you close enough for your water recipe.

In order to make the maths easier later, the best approach is to make two solutions, one of the minerals and one of the buffer, at 1,000ppm (parts per million) concentration. To do this:

- Dissolve 2.45g of Epsom salts per litre of distilled water.
- Dissolve 1.68g of bicarbonate of soda (baking soda) per litre of distilled water.

You can now create a variety of recipes, matching the water from cities around the world or from those with expertise within the coffee industry (such as those shown on the chart on page 45). I would recommend having a look at www.baristahustle.com as it has recipes, recipe calculators and a great deal more information about coffee and brewing.

BOTTLED WATER

It is still fairly common to see recommendations for using different bottled mineral waters for coffee brewing. In the past, I have made that recommendation too. However, I would no longer recommend using bottled water as part of a regular routine for coffee brewing.

Bottled water is a great way to highlight the impact of water. Purchase two very different brands, say Evian and Volvic, and make a brew with each. The difference in your coffee will be very clear.

However, while some mineral water brands and supermarket offerings are actually quite good for coffee (now that you know what to look for on the label), I remain deeply uncomfortable with the waste and environmental impact that results from using bottled water. I can't deny it can be an effective option, and in some cases it might even be cost effective, but I would counsel anyone using it to periodically have a look at the alternatives that may have become available.

Scales

A set of digital kitchen scales, accurate to at least 1g, is an essential part of better coffee brewing. However, it immediately makes coffee brewing seem scientific, fussy and a little pretentious. From my own perspective, I see a set of scales as something that massively simplifies the process of repeatable and easy coffee making.

The alternative to a set of scales, when it comes to ground coffee, is volumetric measurement using scoops. Personally, I dislike them because I don't want to have to think about whether my spoonful is heaped just enough, or if I even have the right kind of spoon. Pouring water by eye is made infuriatingly difficult by coffee's 'bloom' (its expansion and foaming), which relates to how, and how long ago, the coffee was roasted.

Coffee brewing can be simplified down to a recipe, and the frustrating variability of coffee making goes away when you use a recipe accurately. Small variations in how much coffee or water you use will make your final cup taste notably different, surprisingly so. When you're intentionally experimenting with coffee, this is quite a fun aspect. When you just want your first brew of the day to be good, it is maddening.

I find it much harder to guess the amount of ground coffee I need, or amount of water to pour, before I've had a cup of coffee. This seems cruel to me, and so I want all the help I can get and to outsource any thinking too.

Weighing scales allow my pre-caffeine, sluggish brain to easily hit the key points of a recipe and produce great coffee without having to think very much. This is their real value to me, above giving me a platform for experimentation and exploration.

In the past, I recommended small sets of jewellery scales, as these were the cheapest way to get 0.1g accuracy, but now I'd recommend something with a larger footprint. Even if you're just brewing espresso, most coffee scales will fit into your drip tray so you can weigh the espresso as it brews (see How to Make Espresso, pages 183–89), but will accommodate a portafilter (shown opposite) so you can weigh a ground coffee dose as easily as possible. These larger scales will also accommodate most coffee brewers.

The price of kitchen scales has come down and down, and so you can pick up something very cheaply that will be helpful for both coffee and your wider cooking and baking. Many coffee-focused scales are now accurate to 0.1g, and have a timer function too. These features are desirable but not completely essential.

MAX.2000g / 2-200g d=0.1g / 200-500g d=0.5g / 500-2000g d=1g

HARIO

ON/OFF
TARE

START
STOP

Most people have smartphones, which inevitably have timers, though I prefer to try and avoid interacting with my phone in the morning, before I have to.

Smart Scales

Up until now I've only discussed what are often termed 'dumb scales', as a contrast to wifi- or bluetooth-enabled scales that are now widely available and heavily promoted to the home coffee-brewer. I feel like this moniker is wildly unfair as 'dumb scales' really have all the essentials and 'smart scales' are full of add-on features with questionable value.

I think there's some value in collecting, or seeing, the data from smart scales, but only in limited contexts. I don't like having to interact with my phone during coffee brewing, I don't like the pain of pairing a phone to coffee scales, or the maddening experience of diagnosing why that isn't happening when I just want to get on and make my first cup of the day.

My advice to most people is to consider smart scales when they have a feature that solves a very specific problem for them. Most smart scales come with poorly coded and designed apps that offer neither meaningful insight nor appreciable assistance. In some cases these scales have better build quality, or a better water-resistance rating. I use smart scales when collecting data for experiments, but this is only a fraction of my coffee brewing and I can't make a broad recommendation for them for most people.

What many people want is a set of well-built dumb scales that are waterproof, fast and accurate. These last two points are actually in conflict with one another. When scales are taking measurements there is often a lot of noise in their data, for example vibrations coming from the force of the water being poured into the brewer. In order to be accurate, the scale should collect a lot of data, but process it to remove the noise. This makes the responsiveness of the scale a little slower. The faster a scale updates its display, the less accurate it is likely to be. There are improvements happening constantly in this technology, but it is important to point out the difficulty in delivering this, and why accurate, high-priced scales often seem slower than cheaper ones.

A Coffee Grinder

You'll often find that a coffee grinder is the single best investment you can make for better coffee at home. This is for good reason – because it is absolutely true.

If you dig deeper, you'll find experiments that compared pre-ground coffee from a high-end commercial grinder with freshly ground coffee from a cheap home-grinder and found the former tasted better than the latter. It's an interesting experiment but for me misses out on incorporating the reliable pleasure of the smell of grinding coffee before brewing. In addition, it ignores the importance of using the grind adjustment on the grinder to perfectly match the fineness or coarseness of the grounds with the coffee beans you are brewing, and the brew method you are using. (For more detail, see The Universal Theory of Coffee Brewing, pages 88–9.)

Blade grinder

Burr vs Blade

There are two types of coffee grinders: burr grinders and blade grinders. Blade grinders offer the aromatic pleasure of grinding coffee freshly, but their utility is unfortunately limited. A small blade rotates at very high speed inside the grinding chamber, chopping and smashing the beans to pieces. These pieces end up a mixture of sizes, from very fine powder to larger chunks. The only control you have is over how long you run the grinder for, which gives you very little precision. Upgrading to a burr grinder is the single strongest recommendation I will give in this book.

A burr grinder is defined as having two cutting discs inside it. One is fixed and static and the other spins against it, driven by a motor or by hand. If you own a pepper grinder, then you already own a rudimentary burr grinder, and I'd argue that the difference that freshly ground pepper adds to a dish is a tenth of the impact of a good burr grinder on coffee (where coffee is the main ingredient).

When you're choosing a coffee grinder, there are really four aspects of it that you're trying to assess to see if it fits your needs and budget. These are discussed on the following pages.

1. The Burrs

The cutting discs inside the grinder come in two main shapes: flat and conical. Burrs are usually made of metal, though cheaper grinders do use ceramic burrs. You'll see a variety of geometries and patterns in the way the cutting edges are designed. The larger teeth on the inside do the initial breaking of the coffee beans, and as the coffee moves through the burrs toward the outside it is ground incrementally finer until it is small enough to escape through the gap between them. When you adjust a grinder, you're adjusting the gap between the burrs and the size the pieces of ground coffee need to be to leave the grinding chamber. There are a few different mechanisms used by grinders for adjusting the burr distance, but for the user you either rotate a dial on the grinder, or rotate a collar on the body. The mechanisms allow incredibly small adjustments to the grind size.

The current sentiment within the industry is that there are some burrs which are best suited to filter coffee, some that are better suited to espresso, and those that try to bridge the gap between both. If you are early in your coffee journey, then know that these differences are really pretty small and buying a grinder that perhaps leans toward espresso isn't going to make your filter coffee undrinkable.

I'd recommend paying for a grinder with metal burrs if your budget will allow, as the quality of grind is generally better. (Like any rule there are exceptions, but I think this is good guidance.) As grinders get more expensive, one of the things you are paying for is often the burrs. They may be better quality in their manufacture, so more accurately produced, with better longevity.

Flat burrs

Conical burr

Be careful with very cheap grinders that look like burr grinders. These are typically under £50 ($68), and the burrs do not properly cut the coffee but smash and crush it and don't do a great job. There are now reliable electric burr grinders starting at around £100 ($135), which I would recommend. However, these grinders usually cannot grind fine enough for espresso, and espresso-capable grinders are notably more expensive. This is because of one particular component: the motor.

2. The Adjustment Mechanism

As discussed on the previous pages, burr grinders have some sort of mechanism that moves the burrs closer together or further apart, depending on the requirement of the brew method. There are two approaches to the increments of adjustment you can make: stepped and stepless grinders. Stepped grinders have fixed increments in which you can move the burrs. This is often helpful as it gives some guidance about how much to move the burrs as well as making any changes or settings easily repeatable. Though it is worth noting that the size of the steps between each setting is not universal and some grinders will produce a much bigger change to particle size than others with the movement of a single step.

Stepless grinders are often considered preferable, and for espresso brewing are very nearly essential. Espresso requires very small incremental changes in grind size to get the best out of the coffee, and many stepped grinders can move you from too coarse to too fine with their smallest single movement. Stepless grinders do feel a little more finicky and can be frustrating, but most offer some visual guidance or markings on the grinder for what the manufacturer considers a sensibly sized 'step' (as shown below).

3. The Motor

A significant chunk of the price of a coffee grinder is going toward the motor. Grinding coffee requires a reasonable amount of torque and power, and often a cheaper grinder is limited in its performance by its motor. The finer you grind, the more torque the motor needs, and so cheaper grinders are often unable to effectively grind for espresso without jamming. The manufacturer will build the grinder in such a way as to prevent you from setting the grinder too fine.

A more powerful motor is why espresso-capable grinders start at around £200 ($270) and quickly go up in price from there. Even at this price point the motor will run at a very high RPM (revolutions per minute), as a way to build sufficient momentum to be able to achieve the finer grind you need for espresso.

There isn't a huge amount of evidence available on the impact of burr speed on how your coffee tastes, but high-end grinders are often able to grind at a lower RPM, or even a variable RPM in some cases.

4. Single Dose vs Hopper

Historically, grinders for the home have come with a storage hopper on top of the grinder, designed to hold a bag of coffee beans in it. The trend has begun to move away from grinders like this for two reasons: firstly, the concern is freshness. Coffee is best stored in the dark, in a dry and airtight container. Hoppers on grinders don't really meet those requirements. Secondly, the way people drink coffee has also changed. More and more people have two or more different coffees in their cupboards, and emptying hoppers to refill them with something else simply isn't practical. Increasingly, people are putting just a single dose of coffee into the grinder, and grinding that immediately before brewing. This has lead to more grinders coming to market that don't have hoppers or are designed for single-dose grinding. This, in turn, has lead to some focus on retention within the grinder. Every grinder retains some coffee, though within single-dose grinders the goal has been to get as close to zero retention as possible. Historically, grinders with hoppers had less focus on retention in their design because the primary goal was convenience and some consistency. Thinking about how you intend to brew coffee – whether you'll want the flexibility of single dosing easily or not, and whether you're going to be changing the grind setting significantly and often – should inform your decision on which grinder is the best for you.

When you're shopping for a coffee grinder, these are the main things to consider, and so you should have some idea of whether you want to make espresso or not, or might in the future. Then there are other things to think about: aesthetics; noise (both the loudness and pleasing/grating qualities of the sound); and whether or not the product is properly supported by aftersales where you live.

Importing something cheaply is a very tempting option for many people, but I always advocate for equipment that has good support for parts and repair – with coffee grinders and especially for espresso machines (see How to Buy an Espresso Machine, pages 168–77).

Hand Grinders

It would be remiss not to discuss hand grinders. By removing an expensive component it means you can purchase a good burr grinder at a significant discount compared to an electric counterpart. There are a few things to bear in mind though:

Entry-level grinders often have ceramic burrs, though there are plenty of hand grinders now with metal burrs. If you're trying to get quality results at a discount, then go for metal burrs. If you just want to dip a toe into grinding coffee, and see how much of a difference it makes, then an entry-level burr grinder can be had for £25 ($34).

With the cheaper grinders, aside from the burr sets, the compromise is often in the mechanism that keeps the moving burr stable. Often there'll be some wobble through the driveshaft as the grinder turns. This means that you get a varying gap between your burrs and therefore a less uniform grind. Better hand grinders will have better construction in terms of both design and materials to prevent this happening.

You can spend hundreds on a hand grinder, if not thousands in some cases. Build materials, precision of grinder and burr design and manufacture are where you see improvements, and a £250 ($340) hand grinder is often capable of performing as well as a £500-1,000 ($680-

1,360) electric grinder. The compromise is the work you need to do every morning. Grinding coffee by hand requires a fair amount of effort, especially at finer grind settings. Some people deeply enjoy the ritual, the feeling of working a mechanism to produce freshly, very well-ground coffee that they'll enjoy brewing and drinking even more due to the entirety of the process. Then there are people, like me, who find it more work than it is worth – I see the money spent on an electric motor for my grinder completely worthwhile.

Accessories

Up to this point I've covered the essentials, and with the exception of a coffee brewer (which I'll cover in the How to Brew Great Coffee chapter, pages 87–129) there really isn't anything else that is truly essential.

However, now is as good a time as any to discuss a few key pieces of paraphernalia and equipment that may be of interest at some point in your coffee journey.

Coffee Storage

There is a plethora of canisters and other options designed specifically to store your coffee. Improvements in the bag design that much of the speciality coffee industry uses have meant that it is often the easiest and best way to store coffee. If the bag has a zip seal, then you're not going to do much better than that. However, there are times where you may wish to decant a bag into something else, either because it doesn't seal or the bag isn't ideal for dispensing from.

There are three main categories of coffee-storage canisters:

Airtight/valved containers: These are very simple and just seal airtight. Some have a one-way valve in them to allow any CO_2 coming out of the coffee beans to escape, but this isn't essential. You could use a mason jar or Tupperware as much as you could use something designed especially for coffee. If you do use a clear glass or plastic container,

make sure it is kept in the dark because light does accelerate the staling process.

Displacement containers: These have a mechanism to displace most of the air in the container, usually with a tight-fitting lid piece that sits on top of the coffee beans. These don't significantly improve the condition of the coffee over time, certainly not within the timespan of most people's usage of a bag of coffee. They are often well made, and nice to have, and offer an amount of reassurance that the coffee is well stored.

Vacuum containers: These have a mechanism for pulling most of the air out of the container (though by no means all), and do a slightly better job than anything else when it comes to medium- to long-term storage. If you use one with very fresh coffee, don't be concerned if you pull a vacuum and then the next day find it has lost its vacuum. It is more likely CO_2 coming out of the coffee beans under negative pressure than it is air getting back into the container. These are the most expensive containers, but if they fit your budget then they are worth considering if you want to make sure your coffee lasts as long as possible.

Kettles

While a kettle isn't an absolute essential – there are other ways of heating water – kettles do merit a little discussion because there's quite a range of different options for coffee and quite a broad spread of pricing.

Pouring kettles: Often called gooseneck kettles, these are very popular for pour-over brewing and a few other brew methods. Their long, thin spouts allow controlled, slow pouring of hot water and the shape allows you to pour very close to the bed of coffee if you

wish to minimize the turbulence caused as the water falls into the grounds. These were initially very expensive, but prices have come down a long way and if you brew a lot of pour-overs, then I think they're useful and worth considering. The better-made options are able to go directly on to gas, electric or induction hobs so you can heat water in them. Others choose to boil water in a kettle, then quickly decant into the pouring kettle for the brew.

Temperature-controlled pouring kettles: There are a few situations for which these kettles are useful. If you don't have an electric kettle already, then they're certainly convenient. If you are brewing a medium to dark roast, then being able to consistently use lower water temperatures (80–90°C/ 176–194°F) is very useful too.

However, both of these options generally make poor multi-purpose kettles. If your household drinks a lot of tea, then the capacity of these is often quite small. If you don't need a slow, controlled pour of water for immersion-style brews like the French press or AeroPress, then a regular kettle will be fine. As a kind of middle ground there are some conventional kettles available with temperature control, aimed at tea drinkers who want lower temperatures for white, green or oolong teas.

POUR-OVER COFFEE

Pour-over coffee brewing has become incredibly popular. While it has been a part of coffee brewing in homes for decades, it saw a resurgence in speciality cafés from the middle of the 2000s until the early 2010s.

It is a pretty broad category, defined as a kind of percolation-style brew where water is poured over a bed of coffee, usually sitting inside a filter paper within a cone-shaped brewer, and then drips into the cup or carafe below. It is often called drip coffee, a name which is also used for larger scale coffee brewed in cafés.

Pour-over brewing is popular because it is cheap to get started with, brews one or two cups well and has just enough ritual within its process to provide the satisfying feeling that you've truly made your coffee.

There's an ever-increasing range of shapes, styles and options when picking your first pour-over brewer. The good news is that the cheapest offering in each style is usually made of plastic, which performs better than glass, ceramic or metal when it comes to thermal retention and thus (particularly for lighter roasts) is an uncompromised place to start.

Carafes

The last in the group of accessories worth discussing are carafes. These are most definitely not essential, but they are in the 'very nice to have' category. A number of brewers are designed to brew into a single cup, but some can brew more than one serving at a time. In these situations you will want something to brew onto, and most use some sort of carafe for exactly this purpose.

Initially, the limited choice of coffee-focused options meant everything seemed a little expensive. That has now changed and there's a delightful choice out there. Most are glass, which I recommend for no other reason than well-brewed coffee in glass looks wonderful and the reddish hue that you see when it catches the light unquestionably adds a something something to the enjoyment of your morning cup.

I haven't really covered cups, or coffee-specific tasting glassware here. There's too much to explore, and it really belongs in the world of personal preference. The cup you like the look of, the heft of, that brings you a little pleasure is the correct cup for you.

3

HOW TO TASTE COFFEE

One of the quickest ways to get to better-tasting coffee is through trying it, and understanding the root causes of the tastes you like or dislike.

While the idea of making changes through taste can initially seem a bit fuzzy and nebulous, it is effective and ultimately satisfying. When I talk to people about this, many are hesitant because they believe they lack the palate or skills of an experienced taster. With just a little guidance, however, they're often shocked at how accurately they can perceive small changes and can easily see how a change of recipe or technique has made their cup better. Unquestionably, this is a skill that is developed through practice, but just about everyone has the capacity to be a good taster.

The delight of great coffee is its taste, but there is an additional layer of enjoyment when you understand how that great taste is composed, and why and how the coffee tastes as good as it does. To start with I want to quickly break down the mechanics of how you taste and then I'll tie this into coffee more specifically.

The Mouth vs the Nose

The language around tasting can be frustrating. We're taught that there are five basic tastes: sweet, salty, sour, bitter and umami. These are all detected in the mouth through our taste buds.

There are other tastes experienced in the mouth, such as astringency, piquancy, the heat of spicy foods or things that taste metallic. Your taste buds work in a relatively simple way, where different compounds trigger receptors, which in turn trigger nerves to tell your brain that you're experiencing that taste. You'll sometimes see references to a term like 'super taster'. This is someone that has a higher-than-average number of taste buds. To be a super taster is not necessarily a good thing because you'll experience things like saltiness more than other people, so getting seasoning right when cooking for others can be tricky. Often super tasters don't like coffee because they experience its bitterness more intensely than others. However, being a super taster doesn't mean that you have a better palate for experiencing flavours or sensations that are detected away from the taste buds.

If you've ever had a cold, or suffered a loss of smell, then when you've eaten or drunk foods you will still have experienced the basic tastes – though often you're distracted by what is missing: flavour. The complexity of food, the defining character of its flavour, is detected in the olfactory bulb that sits at the top of the nasal cavity. Flavours and aromas come in the form of volatile organic compounds. To break that down a bit, volatile means that they are easily evaporated at normal temperatures, so they are floating around in the air. Organic compounds, from a chemical perspective, are carbon-based compounds likely of a biological origin. Your sense of smell is an astonishing thing. When the olfactory bulb detects a compound like this it is instantly able to determine its smell. What is more astonishing is that it can be a compound never before seen in nature, that's manufactured in a lab, and your nose will instantly know what it smells like and, for example, if it smells woody. On top of that, anyone else smelling it will experience the same thing.

Where taste language gets particularly frustrating is in the difference between taste and flavour. Aroma is something you experience through the nose, by pulling in air full of these volatile organic compounds, as you sniff a cup of coffee before drinking it. When you drink it, you experience some tastes in your mouth and then just as you swallow, you automatically do what's called a swallow breath. Try it now: swallow and then afterwards you'll instinctively blow a little air up and out of your nose. This sends

those same volatile compounds that you were smelling earlier back to the olfactory bulb. However, most people experience a blending of the tastes in their mouth and smells in their nose as a singular moment which is difficult to separate, especially in hindsight.

A very simple way to split apart taste and flavour is something you likely learned in childhood: holding your nose while you eat something you don't like. Pinching your nostrils shut makes the swallow breath ineffective, so those flavours you don't like never really get sent to your olfactory bulb. If you have anything edible to hand, then it is absolutely worth trying this right now. Put the book down, grab the food, pinch your nose, chew for a bit, thinking about what you're experiencing, then open your nose back up. It feels like a black and white film suddenly switches to colour.

In many foods and drinks there are an overwhelming number of different aromatic compounds for your olfactory bulb to contend with. Your brain does a very clever thing by taking in the taste information first and using it as a cue for picking apart the flavours that come next. If the tongue experiences a lot of citric acid, then your brain will be primed to pick out citrus-like aromas. This is why the language used to describe coffee aromas can sometimes be a good guide for how much acidity there will be in the coffee.

What seems to impress people is the ability to taste something and pick apart the different flavours within it, as if the taster is detecting and identifying individual volatile compounds. Sometimes this is actually the case, though really quite rarely. In most cases, this is the taster trying to unpick the combination of tastes and aromas they are experiencing within the context of that food or drink. If someone describes a coffee as tasting of strawberries, that doesn't mean that it has the same volatile compounds as strawberries, nor the same as a wine that a different taster might describe as tasting of strawberries. While there are objective flavours in certain foods, the way different brains assess and decode masses of information is different, and so the experience of flavour is often relatively subjective.

The good news here is that there are no wrong answers. If a cup of coffee has flavours that remind you of watermelon, but no one else gets what you mean, that doesn't make you wrong. Your brain has a unique set of taste experiences and pattern recognition built around your life so far. There are no points in life for being able to describe a coffee or a glass of wine more accurately than another person. The value comes from understanding the tastes that you like, the experiences that you like, and from being able to pay attention to a full spectrum of flavour which makes a great cup of coffee feel complex and, ultimately, beautiful.

THE PLUS SIDE TO BAD COFFEE

There is one particular aspect of learning to taste that I think is worth highlighting. Once you really start to pay attention to flavours, hunt for language and try to paint a linguistic picture of the tasting experience, it is very easy to stop actually enjoying it.

The best analogy I can offer is that it is a bit like cooking food for a dinner party. As you, the cook, start eating you're often actively looking for points of failure. While others around the table compliment the food, all you experience and focus on are the things you did wrong: something might seem overcooked, under- or over-seasoned, you'll think about what could have been better. No one else is really assessing the food in this way, they're experiencing a simpler question: do I like this? Just switch the experience for when someone has cooked for you and clearly been unhappy with the food that you're really enjoying.

It is a fine line to tread; paying attention to something can reveal greater beauty but you can easily begin to focus on its flaws and not its strengths. Personally, I've struggled with this in a cyclical way throughout much of my adult life where conscious tasting has been a part of my job. My best advice is to sometimes eat or drink something that really isn't very good. Bad coffee is broadly available and great for resetting the baseline of your expectations for the coffee you brew or drink. We all need a little ugliness around to be able to see beauty in the world.

Comparative Tasting

Learning to taste coffee, by which I mean learning to understand and pull apart the experience of coffee tasting, is relatively easy to do and is undoubtedly extremely rewarding. To do this in the shortest amount of time, and with the highest return, there is really only one way to approach it: comparative tasting.

Comparative tasting is popular with things like wine or whisky, but still relatively rare in coffee. A comparative tasting, especially with a little guidance, very quickly gives you some insight into what you enjoy and why. This exercise can be done with just two different cups of coffee, though more can help. If you're just starting out, then I wouldn't recommend tasting more than five different things at the same time. It is all too easy to feel overwhelmed and lost in a wine tasting of a dozen different bottles, and the same is true with coffee.

Special, guided note-taking, or scoring sheets, are popular in the coffee industry. I think they can be very useful when adapted to those starting out in the experience, to help provide some framework and a place to capture thoughts. I don't think there's a ton of value in keeping notes on coffee tastings long term – coffee is such a changeable thing that you're unlikely to recapture an old experience. Even if you seek out coffee from the same farm, roasted by the same company, the taste will change somewhat from one year to the next. (Though I accept note taking would allow you to track the changes in a farm's coffee from one year to the next.)

Where to Start

You can do a comparative tasting very easily, and you can adapt it to whatever brewing equipment you have around. In the coffee industry, coffee tasting has to be standardized quite heavily because the goal of the tasting is assessment of the coffee itself. As such, coffee is brewed in a specific way for tasting so it can easily be repeated across multiple brews of multiple coffees. However, if you're just trying to compare two different cups of coffee, then you're not constrained in quite the same way.

Often I recommend finding two French presses and brewing two different coffees in them. However, if you only have one but you have a different brewer, such as a pour-over, then it is perfectly OK to brew one cafetière and compare it to one pour-over. You can do more specific comparative tastings to learn specific things, such as brewing the same coffee using two different brew methods, but for now you just need two cups of coffee that are different. This could be different

Coffee:

	Aroma	Acidity	Sweetness	Body	Finish	Flavour	Overall
Quantity	⊢┼┼┼⊣ Low · High	⊢┼┼┼⊣ Low · High	⊢┼┼┼⊣ Low · High	⊢┼┼┼⊣ Light · Heavy	⊢┼┼┼⊣ Short · Long		/10
Quality	⊢┼┼┼⊣ - · +	⊢┼┼┼⊣ - · +	⊢┼┼┼⊣ - · +	⊢┼┼┼⊣ - · +	⊢┼┼┼⊣ - · +		
Notes							

Coffee:

	Aroma	Acidity	Sweetness	Body	Finish	Flavour	Overall
Quantity	⊢┼┼┼⊣ Low · High	⊢┼┼┼⊣ Low · High	⊢┼┼┼⊣ Low · High	⊢┼┼┼⊣ Light · Heavy	⊢┼┼┼⊣ Short · Long		/10
Quality	⊢┼┼┼⊣ - · +	⊢┼┼┼⊣ - · +	⊢┼┼┼⊣ - · +	⊢┼┼┼⊣ - · +	⊢┼┼┼⊣ - · +		
Notes							

Coffee:

	Aroma	Acidity	Sweetness	Body	Finish	Flavour	Overall
Quantity	⊢┼┼┼⊣ Low · High	⊢┼┼┼⊣ Low · High	⊢┼┼┼⊣ Low · High	⊢┼┼┼⊣ Light · Heavy	⊢┼┼┼⊣ Short · Long		/10
Quality	⊢┼┼┼⊣ - · +	⊢┼┼┼⊣ - · +	⊢┼┼┼⊣ - · +	⊢┼┼┼⊣ - · +	⊢┼┼┼⊣ - · +		
Notes							

Coffee:

	Aroma	Acidity	Sweetness	Body	Finish	Flavour	Overall
Quantity	⊢┼┼┼⊣ Low · High	⊢┼┼┼⊣ Low · High	⊢┼┼┼⊣ Low · High	⊢┼┼┼⊣ Light · Heavy	⊢┼┼┼⊣ Short · Long		/10
Quality	⊢┼┼┼⊣ - · +	⊢┼┼┼⊣ - · +	⊢┼┼┼⊣ - · +	⊢┼┼┼⊣ - · +	⊢┼┼┼⊣ - · +		
Notes							

coffee from different places, or two different roasts of the same coffee, or two different brew methods. The point is simply that they are different and to start out I'd recommend trying to make them as different as possible.

Once your two coffees have brewed, let them cool down a little bit. Even if you enjoy your coffee piping hot, for this exercise you're going to let them cool down until they're warm. The reason is primarily that your sense of taste works much better when the thing it is tasting is close to body temperature. Extremes of hot or cold heavily diminish your ability to taste even the simple flavours. A chilled cola should taste refreshing and balanced, sweet but not too sweet. Taste that same drink at room temperature and the sweetness suddenly seems unpleasantly overwhelming. This is because your mouth can now accurately detect how much sugar is actually in there! The same is true with coffee tasting, and if you taste coffee from hot down to cool you'll experience a kind of 'opening up' of flavour the cooler the cup gets. Often coffee professionals will taste a coffee until it cools to room temperature to make sure they've fully experienced the good and the bad in the cup.

How to Use a Tasting Sheet

Opposite is a tasting sheet to get you started. I like to use this for people starting out as the framework is quite simple. Don't feel that you have to use the note sections for each

category, they're just there in case you want to capture something. And take your time with it. I'd recommend putting aside at least 20 minutes for a tasting like this, because it is astonishing how much your experience of the coffees will change over time, especially as they cool down.

The first section on aroma is optional for your first few tastings. It's there to capture your initial impressions of a cup of coffee, before you start tasting it. The smell of coffee is probably its most enjoyed attribute, a pleasure to those who don't even like the taste. When you smell the cup before drinking, is the aroma intense? Do you like it? Don't worry about trying to describe that smell right now, unless something stands out to you.

To start your tasting, you are going to focus on one single aspect of the coffee's taste. In this example we'll take acidity. Acidity is one of the more challenging aspects of coffee. Some people love the brightness, the crispness and juiciness that it brings to coffee. Others find it unpleasant. In this moment you're not going to focus on how much you like it, you're just going to try and pay attention to how acidic the first cup is and then compare that to the second cup. Which one is more acidic? Is there a big difference or is it subtle? Does the acidity feel the same? Then you can start to think about whether it is sour and harsh, or refreshing and pleasant. On the sheet you'll see that with acidity you can note down how much there is, but also how much you like it. With things like acidity, for some people more is not always better.

You can bounce between the two cups, focusing on just one aspect. Once you feel like you've got your head around the difference, then start to focus on a different attribute: which cup feels sweeter? Then you can focus on the body (sometimes described as the mouthfeel) of the two cups. Does one feel fuller and heavier and the other lighter?

Finish is about how the coffee leaves your mouth feeling when you swallow. Does the coffee linger, or does it seem to disappear? Does it leave a pleasant sensation or are you reaching for a glass of water to clear the taste? Then you can move on to flavour.

The trick with flavour is to start out using broad categories. No one is expecting you to jump to highly specific terms straight away (though if a particular word jumps out at you, then note it down). Does the coffee have a fruitiness to it? Does it have a nutty or chocolatey quality? Does it just taste like the roasted flavours of coffee? Once you've got a broad category in mind, then you can start to drill down. If it is fruity, then what kind of fruit does it remind you of? Is it the tartness of citrus fruits? Is it the crispness of apples? Does it make you think of berries? You can keep drilling down into a category as far as you like, and wine or coffee flavour wheels exist as guides for this particular process. Some people find these harder to use, and want to reach straight for some sort of specific descriptor, and there's no issue with that. You also don't have to use any specific language either. One of the enduring descriptors someone used at a tasting described a coffee as 'late-career Marlon Brando', which communicated quite a lot in a surprising and accurate way!

Tasting Takeaways

At the end of the tasting it is worth thinking more about which coffees you liked and why. What did you enjoy about a coffee? The more often you taste this way, the more you understand the taste profile of what you enjoy, and this helps to improve your hit rate of buying coffee you really enjoy drinking each morning. As an added bonus, comparative

tastings are always fun and the process can bring a new element of delight to any food or drink you already enjoy, be it chocolate or cheese, and can help you craft better recipes in the kitchen too. I know people who've been working in coffee for 40 years who still haven't tired of comparative tasting.

SHARING NOTES

If you're going to taste with someone else, and I highly recommend including friends or family in the fun, then while you're tasting I'd advise you not to talk about what you're experiencing. Someone saying a descriptor out loud can lead to a kind of bias where everyone else looks for that specifically and it becomes harder to taste anything else. Even experienced tasters are highly suggestible. However, once you've finished tasting, then I'd absolutely recommend comparing notes and talking about the ways you agree or disagree and continuing to taste as you do this. As discussed on pages 74–5, your brain will pick apart and put back together the experience of a cup of coffee in a different way to someone else, and so no one is having the 'correct' experience or writing down the 'right' words.

HOW TO BREW GREAT COFFEE

For as long as people have been drinking coffee they've been experimenting with ways to brew it. There have been countless coffee-brewing inventions, and a surprising number have found popularity. This means that if you want to talk about how to make better-tasting coffee, you need to think about how that might apply to an AeroPress as much as a French press.

I'll cover the details and step-by-steps for a number of different brewers in this section, but before that I'll talk about the more universal aspects of coffee brewing. That way, should you find yourself facing down something you've never seen before, something not covered here, you'll stand a very good chance of making good coffee with it very quickly.

More than that, it never hurts to reiterate the important idea that there is no one right way to make coffee. There are times that it is fun to play around, to try new things, new techniques or ideas. What I'm going to present are techniques that should get you to great coffee with as little fuss or unnecessary work as possible. I hope they'll be your base techniques, and with a growing understanding of coffee brewing you'll feel comfortable riffing or changing them up when the mood takes you. And when you just want a coffee, fall back on them and get to delicious every time.

The Universal Theory of Coffee Brewing

This chapter is designed to give you an understanding of the underlying *how* and *why* of brewing great coffee. The principles here apply to every method of brewing coffee so, while this is at the start of the section covering coffee brewing, I would recommend reading this even if you're just going to be making espresso.

The process of roasting coffee completely transforms the raw seeds of the coffee plant. Alongside the creation of the smells and aromas that are the backbone of an enjoyable and interesting cup, the coffee bean becomes both brittle and porous. When you break it into pieces, you expose more of its surface area, and that surface area is primarily what determines how much flavour you get from it when you brew. This next section involves some light maths (everyone's favourite!) but understanding this can really help with making a better cup of coffee, or understanding why a cup might be bad.

Understanding Extraction

In typical ground coffee nearly 70 per cent is insoluble, so you could brew a batch of grounds endlessly and there will still be some spent grounds to throw away afterwards. What can be dissolved into water are the compounds that make up coffee's flavour in the cup. Theoretically your maximum extraction was thought to be around 30 per cent of the coffee you brew with.

The coffee industry used to talk about a certain range of extraction being ideal: 18–22 per cent was considered a good target for a good-tasting cup. It can be an abstract thing to think about, so let's put some numbers behind it.

Let's say you brew a pour-over with 30g of coffee, using 500g of water and in doing so you extract 20 per cent of the coffee. If you took your spent grounds and dried them very slowly in the oven until all the retained water was gone, then they'd now only weigh 80 per cent of their initial weight: 24g. The brew of coffee contains the missing 6g of coffee, now dissolved in the liquid, giving it colour, aroma and flavour.

In the past, this is pretty much how measurement was done: oven-drying of ground coffee being the technique used to develop the target range of coffee extraction. However, in the last decade or so that has been replaced by the modern technology of using a refractometer (an instrument that can measure the concentration in a liquid) to measure the liquid coffee. This means that we can now convert the refractive index of the coffee to an expression of strength.

In the example on the previous page, the refractometer might show a strength of 1.36 per cent. If you weigh your liquid coffee (you can't use the 500g you started with because some of that water has been absorbed by the ground coffee) and you have 440g, then it is easy to calculate how much coffee you extracted (440 × 1.36 = ~6g). Thus your extraction percentage is 6g/30g (your starting dose of grounds), which is 20 per cent.

You could always dehydrate your cup of coffee, and measure what is left. This is, in a much more simplified way, how instant coffee is made. Your teaspoon of instant coffee is pure, soluble coffee material that has been brewed and then freeze-dried, formed into attractive little clumps, which look a bit like fresh coffee grounds, then packaged and sold.

Measuring extraction is primarily the concern of the coffee industry; it is used for research and development, diagnostics or helping standardize drinks in a café. However, this understanding is useful because of terms that are extremely important and commonly used: underextraction and overextraction.

Underextraction and Overextraction

Underextraction was previously defined as a brew of coffee where the total extraction was below the target window, and overextraction was when the total extraction exceeded the window. A deeper understanding of what is happening in coffee brewing has led to a reassessment of how we use those terms and what they really mean.

The flaw in the simple definitions of under- and overextraction is that they don't really help us understand *why* a brew might taste bad. In the past, the solution to underextraction was to grind finer, and conversely to grind more coarsely for an overextracted cup. This approach seems reasonable at first – the coarser a coffee is ground, the less total surface area there is, so the less access water has to the flavours in the ground coffee. Frustratingly, in the real world it didn't solve our problematically bad cups of coffee in the way that we would have liked.

Grind Size Guide

Espresso

Moka/AeroPress

Filter coffee

French press

Batch brew

When Coffee Tastes Bad

It is useful to talk about the flavours associated with under- and overextraction. Underextracted coffee generally tastes quite thin, with a dominant and unpleasant acidity or sourness. Overextracted coffee has an intense bitterness, astringency and an unpleasant aftertaste.

The mistake that many have made over the years is to treat ground coffee as a homogenous thing that either gives up too little or too much flavour. In many cases bad coffee happens because some of the coffee doesn't give up enough flavour and some gives up too much. One of the aspects of the brewing techniques throughout the book, that will come up again and again, is the idea of trying to extract your coffee as evenly as possible.

The chase for evenness is the rabbit hole that people fall down, which initially is a great return on investment but can end up being a chase for optimization which explains why they might spend thousands on coffee grinders, brewers or espresso machines. Like many things in life, coffee is pretty easy to get good at. You can make delicious coffee easily with some simple techniques, but if you're chasing the last 2 or 3 per cent of excellence, then the learning curve is much steeper. Chasing down these last few incremental improvements isn't worth it to many people, but to some it brings great pleasure – though often at expense to their wallet.

Evenness isn't just about *how* you brew, but also about *what* you brew. Having coffee grounds in a huge range of sizes makes achieving evenness very difficult. Blade grinders (see page 54) produce such a range of pieces that it is pretty much impossible to get a truly even brew from the grounds – though with a few little tips and tricks you can get some good results.

The picture opposite shows how different grind sizes suit certain brew methods. We'll go into more detail on different brewers in the next chapter, but it is worth remembering that whatever size you are grinding to, the key is that the grind size is even.

How to Control Extraction

There are two primary ways to change the extraction of ground coffee: change the way the coffee is ground and adjust the amount of water that you use to brew. I'll discuss these first, and then get into a few of the other key variables.

Water isn't particularly good at getting at flavours inside coffee grounds, it really is mostly just washing away whatever is exposed on the surface of the particles. The finer you grind a fixed amount of coffee, the more surface area you expose. In an ideal world this would be the only variable you'd need to work with, but as you get finer and finer it gets more difficult to separate coffee grounds from the finished beverage. If you're using a filter paper, then gravity will start to struggle to get the liquid to flow through grounds so fine they're acting as a sandbag. The worst-case scenario here is that water finds a pathway, a channel, through the grounds and more water flows through this channel compared to the rest of the bed. This would mean that any coffee grounds along this channel would be extremely extracted – overextracted – and that the remaining coffee would be underextracted, having seen less than its share of brewing water.

This brings us to the second key variable: the amount of water that you brew with. In coffee brewing, water acts as a solvent for flavour. The more solvent you use, the more flavour you are going to dissolve. For example, if you brewed two French presses and kept the coffee identical in both and added more water to one than the other, then the larger brew would be weaker, but if you measured the extraction you'd see that it had extracted more soluble material from the grounds. In a pour-over it seems more obvious that if you use more water to brew with, then you'll extract more flavour; you can see that the additional brewed liquid that falls from the base of the cone has colour and flavour and so is pulling more from the grounds.

If someone has great coffee, good clean water and has ground the coffee using a burr grinder (see page 54) but is having bad results, then probably 75 per cent of the time it is one of these two variables that is causing the issue. This is why scales are so useful in coffee brewing (see page 53), as they let you know and control key aspects of your coffee.

Temperature

A lot is made of the impact of temperature on coffee brewing, and while it does have a definite and important effect, it is probably a little overstated.

The hotter your water is, the more coffee/flavour it is going to extract, and in some cases this isn't desirable. Lighter roasts are less soluble than darker roasts, and darker roasts also contain more bitter-tasting compounds. If you brew dark roasts with very hot water, you'll have an intense and quite bitter cup. As such I'd recommend using boiling – or close-to-boiling – water for very light roasts, and then water at 90–95°C (194–203°F) for medium roasts and at 80–90°C (176–194°F) for dark roasts. This refers to the temperature of the water in the kettle, as the temperature during brewing in a French press or pour-over is usually quite a bit lower than the temperature of the kettle.

WATER TEMPERATURE FOR DIFFERENT ROASTS

Very light roasts: 95–100°C (203–212°F)

Light roasts: 92–100°C (198–212°F)

Medium roasts: 85–95°C (185–203°F)

Medium-dark roasts: 80–90°C (176–194°F)

Dark roasts: 80–85°C (176–185°F)

Evenness

This isn't really a variable you should be playing with, more a variable outcome of your brewing.

Evenness is about having the coffee grounds all interact with a roughly equal amount of water. In practice, to have it be truly uniform isn't possible. Coffee will always break and shatter during grinding to produce a range of particle sizes, even with the nicest and most expensive coffee grinders and burr sets. You can still get incredibly enjoyable cups, and you can try to quiet the voice in your head that might ask 'but what if it was even more uniform?'

When you're practising a brewing technique, or experimenting with a new idea, then it is worth bearing in mind how this change or procedure might influence the evenness of your brew. More even brews tend to taste sweeter, mostly due to having less distractions from the sweetness of the coffee, less sourness, less astringency, less bitterness. I am not trying to encourage people too deep down this rabbit hole. Mostly this kind of thinking is for the moments when your brew is clearly flawed and you're trying to understand why.

Using those key tastes of bitterness and sourness to guide you, adjusting by taste is always going to be more important than going by readings like refractometer readings (see pages 88–9) because the point of brewing coffee is to drink it, not to have it pass a technical exam. If it brings you delight, if you are a little bit sad that the cup has finished, then it is OK to just enjoy it and shoot for the same thing the next time you brew, without having to pick it apart to try and endlessly iterate it to somehow make it better. This thinking can be challenging but also a thief of joy, and no one wants that from their morning brew.

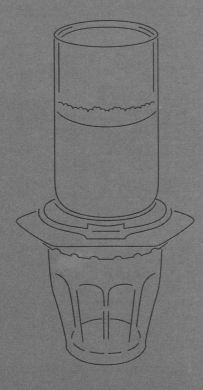

How to Get The Best From Your Brewer

French Press

The press-pot brewer (or French press) is, I believe, underrated, but is thankfully extremely popular.

While it may languish, collecting dust, in many people's cupboards, this is a wonderfully simple way to prepare coffee. The history of the brewer is a little confusing, especially as it is most commonly known as the French press. The first patented design for a brewer like this dates back to 1852, and two Frenchmen named Mayer and Delforge. However, this design had no commercial success. The patent of Attilio Calimani in 1929 is generally seen as the birth of the brewer, which is confusing as Calimani was Italian. The brewer first became popular in France, and was known as the Chambord, and was marketed in England as La Cafetière. Both are brands that exist today.

How to Brew

Suggested ratio: 60–70g/litre
Grind size: Medium to medium-fine
Buying advice: The iconic cafetière is glass, and most of the presses available are glass bodied. However, for a couple of reasons I'd recommend stretching to a dual-walled, stainless-steel version if your budget allows. Primarily, I recommend these because they're unbreakable and glass most definitely is not. More expensive glass options generally have better and stronger glass, but a stainless-steel version will last a lifetime. Secondly, for those with a concern about the loss in temperature with a longer brew time, like the one I recommend, a dual-walled, stainless-steel press will retain the heat much better than glass.

Some people do say they can taste something 'off' or metallic with stainless-steel brewers, but in blind testing I've never been able to detect any difference. However, it is possible some people have a particular sensitivity that I do not.

Maintenance: Soap and water should be used after every brew. If for any reason you start to get a brown patina building up on the brewer, then dissolve about 1 tablespoon (10g) of espresso-machine cleaner (I use Cafiza, but other brands also work well) per litre of very hot water and soak for a few hours before rinsing thoroughly.

STEP BY STEP

1 Grind your coffee just before brewing. Place the press on the scales and put your ground coffee into the press. Zero the scales.

2 Boil your water and, depending on your desired brew temperature (see page 94), pour the required amount over the coffee. Leave the press for 4 minutes.

3 Take a large spoon and stir the crust that has formed on top gently.

4 Using two large spoons, scoop off any foam and floating ground coffee.

Wait for 3–5 minutes, depending on your preference and on how much of rush you're in. The longer, the better. This will allow more of the grounds, especially the fine pieces, to sink to the bottom of the brewer.

▶ Dialling It In

The joy of the French press is how good a job it does of brewing coffee, with the bare minimum of technique. The technique opposite is more about reducing silt in the cup rather than worrying about evenness of extraction or tweaking the brewing process. Infusion/immersion brewing like this is generally extremely good at even brewing and your extraction will usually be pretty good across a range of grind sizes. Coarser grind sizes can and should be steeped for longer, but go too fine and it becomes harder to get a sediment-free cup. If the cup is weak and on the acidic side in an unpleasant way, then I'd recommend grinding a little finer the next time. If the cup is a bit too strong, or a touch too bitter, then going a little coarser on your grind size will balance things out.

Some people like to enhance the texture of a good French press which comes, in part, from using a metal filter rather than paper or cloth and thus allows more oil and tiny suspended pieces of coffee to end up in your brew. You can do this with slightly higher doses of coffee (more like 70g/litre), but I would be hesitant to do this to fix a brew that isn't quite right. Only adjust your dose when you're brewing a cup you like a lot, but want to be a little more intense.

5 Insert the press mechanism and press until the mesh is on the very top of the liquid coffee.

At no point should you plunge the press to the bottom. Plunging will churn up all the sediment in the brewer, that you've been waiting to settle to the bottom, meaning you'll get that unwanted chalky sediment in your cup.

6 Pour gently. To avoid as much sediment as possible, keep an eye on the spout as the coffee pours and stop before pouring the very last of the liquid once you see a lot more sediment in the liquid.

Drink and enjoy.

V60

This is probably the brewer most associated with the modern speciality coffee movement.

You'll see it in both homes and businesses, and it could well be considered an essential basic item of brewing. This cone-shaped brewer made by Hario, in Japan, takes its name from the angle of its walls. It is a simple brewer, easy to use and capable of excellent results. It is also a relatively late entrant into the home brewer market, being released in 2004 – though the company itself dates back to 1921.

The method here is about getting key things right: getting all the coffee brewing at the same time; pouring in a way that agitates the bed of coffee just the right amount; and making sure that you have an even brew with a nice flat bed of spent coffee at the end.

I use a lot of different brewers, but the V60 is a great benchmarking tool for me. Paper filters give me great clarity, it is easy to brew consistently and it tends to encourage you to grind a bit finer, which I generally enjoy. Here are some key tips and techniques to make sure you're getting the best out of it. It might seem a bit fussy on the first read through, but it isn't. It's just about focusing on the key things.

How to Brew

Suggested ratio: 60g/litre
Grind size: Medium to medium-fine
Buying advice: Definitely grab a plastic cone to start with. They're the cheapest, but have better heat retention and brew as well or better than the glass, metal or ceramic options.

When it comes to choosing papers, you should know that these can have a big impact on brewing time. Hario has several different paper suppliers across its different paper filter range, and some papers brew faster than others. There are also many third party manufacturers who make excellent papers. Above all I'd recommend using the white, bleached filters and not the brown, unbleached filters. The unbleached can impart a papery taste to your coffee, which a lot of people don't like.

The V60 Brewing Table

This brewing method works best when using two main pours, and the size of these is relative to the size of the brew you are making. Here's a little table breaking down some common brew sizes.

IMPORTANT: These numbers are the **total cumulative weights**, not individual pours. Essentially these are the numbers you want to see on the scale while you're making coffee.

Coffee dose		15g		20g		30g	
Time (m)	Phase	Water added (g)	Cumulative brew weight (g)	Water added (g)	Cumulative brew weight (g)	Water added (g)	Cumulative brew weight (g)
0:00–0:45	Bloom	30–40	30–40	40–50	40–50	60–80	60–80
0:45–1:15	Pour one	110–120	150	150–160	200	220–240	300
1:15–1:45	Pour two	100	250	130	330	200	500

STEP BY STEP

1 Rinse your filter with hot water. Hot water from the tap is OK, if your water gets nice and hot. This not only rinses out any papery taste from the paper, but also heats the brewer up. The lighter the roast of the coffee you are brewing, the hotter you'll want things to be.

Place your brewer on a cup or carafe.

Grind your coffee just before brewing. Pour into the middle of the cone, and make a small, volcano-like well in the centre using your finger or a spoon.

2 Boil your water, and use right from the boil. Gently pour a little water on to the coffee. You're trying to just wet all the grounds, so that they swell and release CO_2. This phase is called the bloom. Generally aim to use 2g of water per gram of coffee, but you can use a little more if you need to get more coffee wet.

3 As soon as you've poured the water, pick up the brewer and swirl it around in a circular motion. You are trying to get absolutely all the coffee mixed with the water. If you see lumps or big bubbles forming, swirl a little more.

Leave the coffee to sit for around 45 seconds. It will swell like resting dough during this time, and don't worry if some water is dripping through.

4 Now pour the first main pour. You aim is to take about 30 seconds to pour this stage, and at the end of that time for 60 per cent of the total water to have been poured. The cone should be pretty full at this point, unless you're brewing a single cup in a two-cup brewer. Pour in a gentle, circular motion to make sure water is evenly distributed.

▶ Dialling It In

The main area you'll focus on, once your pouring technique is solid, is the grind. Many people are surprised at how fine you can, and should, grind for a good brew on a V60. I would recommend initially going a little finer each time until suddenly you notice the brew has become a little harsh and bitter, with an unpleasant aftertaste. This happens very suddenly, and is the sign you've gone too fine. Going back just a little coarser will leave you in a sweet spot.

It is worth tracking your brew times, just to see if they're suddenly shifting. This can happen when you change a coffee, and can give you some indication of which way to grind (i.e. coarser or finer) to get a better cup the next time you brew. Due to the variance in papers available, and their impact on brewing time, I can only offer a very rough time window of 3–4½ minutes. Don't worry too much about it. The grind of the coffee and the pouring technique will be what mostly determines extraction, and a variance in brew time due to the papers slowing the flow of water through them doesn't make a massive difference to the taste of the coffee.

5 The next stage is another slow pour, aiming to take another 30 seconds to get all the remaining water in. A gentle circular pour works well here also.

Once you've finished pouring, grab a spoon (tea, soup or dessert – any will work) and give it a circular stir in one direction and then a gentle stir in the opposite direction. This helps prevent any grounds from sticking to the walls of the brewer.

6 When the brewer is drained to about two-thirds full, pick it up and give it a gentle swirl. Again, this helps prevent the coffee from sticking to the walls, and also helps the settled coffee bed end up nice and flat. This will help with evenness

Allow it to drain fully, discard the paper and coffee and enjoy the delicious brew you've made.

The Melitta

Melitta Bentz, after whom the dripper and the company that makes it are named, was the pioneer of paper-filtered, pour-over coffee brewing.

How to Brew

Suggested ratio: 60g/litre
Grind size: Medium to medium-fine
Buying advice: Interestingly this brewer shape is probably more common in automatic coffee brewers than it is in stand-alone, pour-over brewers. Melitta and a few other companies make drippers in this shape, and you can find them in plastic as well as ceramic. The plastic ones tend to feel extremely thin and flimsy, and so while they likely perform well in terms of thermal retention they don't feel like items that are delightful to own. The ceramic versions are usually very nice and easy to recommend. I often recommend using Filtropa papers with these drippers, though the Melitta ones also work well.

Bentz's original invention was a paper-filtered circular dripper, patented in 1908. In 1936 Melitta released the conical shape brewer and matching filter papers and the design hasn't changed very much since then. The Melitta corporation is responsible for various innovations, including the oxygen bleaching process in 1992, to produce white paper filters. This process is now commonly used by many manufacturers.

Technique Variation

Honestly, not much variation is necessary from the V60 technique (see pages 104–5). The Melitta dripper has a smaller open area in its base to let liquid through, so with the same grind size and pour time, the overall brew time will be slightly slower than with a V60 – though the papers do also play a role in this. Let taste guide you in making small adjustments to grind.

Kalita

The Kalita is the most iconic of the flat-bottomed brewers.

This is still the most commonly used flat-bottomed brewer, and Kalita's wave-style filters are also the default for many when it comes to choosing papers for their brewer. Kalita is not the only company that makes a flat-bottomed brewer now; the style has gained a great deal of popularity in the last decade in particular. Many feel that a flat bed of coffee, similar in shape to those you'd find in high-end commercial brewers, do a better job of even extraction. There are pros and cons with every brewer, in terms of technique and ease, so I'd be hesitant to proclaim one style of dripper superior to others.

How to Brew

Suggested ratio: 60g/litre
Grind size: Medium to medium-fine
Buying advice: The metal Kalita models are popular and generally pretty affordably priced. However, there are now a number of similar brewers, with variations on the dimensions or exact design, available from companies such as Espro, Fellow and April. They are all capable brewers, though be aware that the filter papers for these may not be universal, so potentially neither cheap nor easy to acquire.

Technique Variation

A couple of aspects of the V60 technique (see pages 104–5) don't work quite as well: the swirling of the bloom, and the second swirl at the end of the pouring. This is because the wave shape of the paper prevents the movement of liquid. Flat-bottomed brewers benefit from a good pouring kettle more than any of the other brewers discussed. How you pour for the bloom, and how you pour during brewing are key here as you are chasing evenness of water distribution. Slow, steady and circular pours on to the coffee are necessary. Try to pay attention to where you're pouring, making sure you don't leave one part of the coffee bed out.

Chemex

The Chemex brewer was invented in 1941 by Dr Peter Schlumbohm, a German chemist and serial investor who emigrated to the United States, drawn in part by its patent laws.

Schlumbohm patented over 300 different ideas and devices, and the Chemex brewer is unquestionably the most successful and enduring. Its iconic design is made from a single piece of glass and originally had a wood collar held on with a tie. It is a charming brewer, not without its quirks, though much of its character in the cup comes from the very thick paper filters the company also produces.

How to Brew

Suggested ratio: 60g/litre
Grind size: Medium
Buying advice: There are two designs of the traditional shape, one with a wood collar and one with a glass handle. It is hard to pick one – the wood looks nicer, but is annoying to remove and replace for cleaning. The glass version is simpler to clean but the handle is fragile and it tends to live a shorter life. Avoid the small version: I've struggled to get the same cup quality from it and its proportions aren't as beautiful either.

Technique Variation

This isn't so much a variation of the V60 technique (see pages 104–5), but more a couple of pitfalls to be aware of. The filter papers are much thicker than other brewers, which means longer brew times, so I'd grind just a little bit coarser than I would for other pour-over brewers. Secondly, the paper may stick to the glass and also into the pouring funnel. If this happens, the brew will stall as air is unable to escape the bottom of the brewer and creates back pressure on the liquid in the filter. Make sure the funnel is clear, though you can also brew with a chopstick or similar in the funnel to prevent this, as shown here.

Clever Dripper

The Clever Dripper was patented in 1997 in Taiwan but wouldn't really see wider success for at least a decade.

The principle of the brewer is very simple. It is a large Melitta-shaped, conical dripper, but at the base of the brewer there is a stopper. With the dripper sitting on the counter, or on a scale, the stopper is closed. When you place the dripper on to a mug, there is a mechanism that pushes the stopper up, releasing any coffee brewing in the dripper. This allows for a technique that is a mixture of infusion and percolation brewing. While the stopper is closed, the coffee and the water are steeping very evenly and, with good technique, you can follow this phase with even percolation and get a great cup of coffee very easily, without the need for pouring kettles and without much time spent actively involved with brewing. It's a relaxing and satisfying way to brew a cup.

How to Brew

Suggested ratio: 60g/litre
Grind size: Medium-fine
Buying advice: There are other steep-and-release brewers on the market. The Hario V60 Switch is an interesting alternative, but has a smaller capacity. There are a variety of tea brewers that work the same way, but I wouldn't recommend using those. Clever do offer a few variations of their brewer, but I'd just stick with the classic choice. It's inexpensive, reliable, robust and easy to use.

This brew method is focused on making sure you have a good even extraction, and also on the final phase where the liquid drains out of the brewer (often referred to as the 'draw-down') being quick. With other techniques many people have good-tasting coffee, but that phase can stall, adding 5 unnecessary minutes to the brew time.

STEP BY STEP

1

2

3

4

1 Rinse the paper with hot water, and make sure the brewer is completely drained.

Place the brewer on the scales and zero the weight. Do NOT add coffee yet.

2 Boil the water and add your desired amount for your ratio. Note: the brewer can, at a push, accommodate 500g of hot water. I would not recommend brewing with more than 450g of water for risk of spilling. In this example we'll use 300g of water.

3 As soon as possible, add your desired amount of coffee. In this example, add 18g of coffee.

4 Stir the coffee into the water gently, until all the coffee is wet and no dry pockets of grounds remain.

Wait 2 minutes. This can be extended if you're using coarser coffee and you have no control over the grind.

5

6

▶ Dialling It In

Primarily you're going to focus on your grind setting to improve the cup you're getting, though you can also play with brew temperature (see page 94) to correspond with the roast level you are using. If you are not getting a flat bed at the end of the brew, or you can see a lot of unevenness in the bed at the end, then the issue is how you're stirring. Don't be too aggressive or try to create a whirlpool effect. Also make sure the brewer is always resting on a completely flat surface until you transfer it to a cup.

5 Stir the coffee gently.

Wait approximately 30 seconds.

6 Place the brewer on the cup or on to a carafe if you're planning on sharing.

Allow to drain completely. You should have a flat bed of coffee remaining.

Discard the paper, drink and enjoy the coffee.

AeroPress

The AeroPress is a fascinating brewer, reaching iconic status relatively early in its lifetime.

Released originally in 2005, it is the invention of Alan Adler who had already seen success with the Aerobie flying ring. Alan's background was in aerodynamics so his decision to invent a coffee brewer seems somewhat surprising. He was driven to create it because he felt frustrated at how hard it was to brew a single cup of coffee that tasted good with most domestic brewers, which were designed to brew a pot. What he created initially struggled to find a place in the coffee industry but, as single-cup brewing boomed in cafés from around 2008, the product began to take off and has since sold millions of units around the world.

What makes the AeroPress so interesting is that I've always seen such a high level of satisfaction for people who start brewing with it. For many people it is their first single-cup brewer, and the process is fun and the resulting cup notably better than what they'd been drinking before. Many continue to experiment further, both with the AeroPress itself as well as with more brew methods and equipment.

The design is also notable for making it relatively easy to experiment with the variables of coffee brewing. Being able to shift just one aspect – be it grind, brew time or water temperature – without changing much about the rest of the brew allows a deeper understanding of coffee brewing but also encourages experimentation. As such, there are more brewing recipes available online for the AeroPress than any other brewer.

When creating a recipe for the AeroPress (see overleaf), I wanted to achieve a few things. To strip it back to the essentials that impact the cup and for it to be easy and repeatable. Treat this as a trusty everyday recipe, but don't be afraid to stray or experiment with approaches or techniques.

How to Brew

Suggested ratio: 55–60g/litre
Grind size: Medium-fine
Buying advice: There's only one company that makes the original AeroPress, though there are increasing copycats available online. I'd recommend purchasing the original for a few reasons: it is an inexpensive brewer to start with, and saving 10–20 per cent of the purchase price doesn't make sense when you don't have the quality control of construction or materials. AeroPress has been BPA free for a long time, and you can trust that they're using the materials they say they are. It's also important to support inventors properly, even if that involves paying a small premium.

STEP BY STEP

1 Place the filter paper in the holder. Do not rinse, as it doesn't make much of a difference due to there being such a small mass of paper.

Lock the paper holder on to the brewer and place on top of a cup or carafe.

Put everything on a weighing scale.

Add the coffee. In this example we'll use 11g of coffee.

Zero the scales.

2 Pour your water on to the coffee, making sure to get all the coffee wet as you do so. In this example we'll use 200g of water.

3 Place the plunger piece into the brewer, but do not press down. Having the plunger in the top forms a partial vacuum, preventing any further liquid from escaping from the bottom of the brewer.

Wait 2 minutes.

4 Holding both the brewer and the plunger, lift slightly, then gently swirl the brewer. This helps break the crust that has formed in the brewer, and causes most of the coffee to fall to the bottom. Do not swirl aggressively or try to firm a whirlpool. It is just about breaking the crust.

Move the brewer and cup/carafe off the scales.

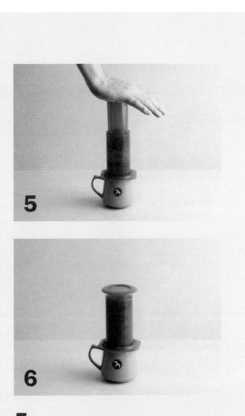

5 Thirty seconds after swirling you can begin to press. Press gently; you should not use any body weight, just a comfortable pressing with the arm.

Pressing should take around 30 seconds (don't worry if there's some variance here - slower is better though).

6 Press until the plunger is on the coffee and can go no further.

Pull the plunger back very slightly before removing, as this helps reduce dripping from the brewer.

Empty the puck (the term for used coffee grounds, as they will often stick together in a solid round puck shape), clean the brewer, drink and enjoy.

▶ A Note on Bypass Brewing (Brewing for Two)

One of the most common criticisms of the AeroPress is that it only makes coffee for one person at a time. But it is possible to brew coffee for two people, by using more coffee and diluting the stronger brew in a carafe before serving.

I'd recommend the same overall technique as opposite but with a few additional points of concern.

1. When brewing this way you want to use as much water in the brewer as possible, to make sure the extraction is effective. In my experience you can use 22g of coffee with up to 240g of water.
2. A longer steep time helps offset having less water in the brewer per gram of coffee. I'd recommend 4 minutes.
3. Add the missing 160g of hot water afterwards.
4. This is also an excellent way to make iced coffee, brewing on to 160g of ice. This should mostly melt when cooling the drink and it can then be served on ice.

▶ Dialling It In

Dialling in an AeroPress can easily feel overwhelming because of the opportunity for endless tweaking of the variables. However, it should be easy to get a good brew relatively easily. This is primarily going to be about grind size, and you might be surprised how fine you can go with this and still have very tasty results. I wouldn't recommend getting into espresso-fine territory, but not far away. Some grinders mark this area as being suitable for Moka-pot brewing (though I recommend a different approach, see pages 124–7).

Be wary of pressing too hard when brewing. In testing it was difficult to get a good brew when pressing hard.

Brew temperature has historically been an area of focus, especially as Alan Adler advocates brewing at 80°C (176°F). Brewing at that lower temperature does work well across a surprising range of coffees, but I'd still advocate matching your brew temperature to the coffee roast level and going all the way up to boiling point with lighter roasts (see page 94).

Siphon Brewer

The siphon brewer is a surprisingly old brewing technology.

Despite being more strongly associated with Asian manufacturers like Hario in Japan and Yama in Taiwan, the siphon brewer originated in Europe. The first versions, often called vacuum pots, appeared in Germany in the 1830s and the first commercial success belongs to a Frenchwoman named Jeanne Richard in 1838, which referenced an earlier design by Loeff of Berlin.

The idea behind the brewer is relatively simple, though exceedingly pleasing in execution. As water boils in the bottom chamber of the brewer, it is trapped and forces the water up a tube into the top section. As long as heat is applied to the bottom chamber, then the water will stay in the top chamber and maintain a pretty steady temperature. You can add ground coffee to the water and then let it steep. To end the brew the heat is removed from the base and, as it cools, the steam condensing causes a mild vacuum that pulls the water back down from the top chamber through the coffee, which is trapped against a filter of some sort – usually cloth tied around a metal disc.

This is a theatrical, engaging but challenging brewer. It is easy to make pretty terrible coffee with it, and the brewing procedure makes regular use frustrating unless you build a routine and process around it. The brewer briefly enjoyed a resurgence around 2009–2012, when by-the-cup brewing was fashionable in modern coffee shops. It is now relatively rare to see one in a coffee shop, though that doesn't mean you shouldn't seek it out if you're visiting somewhere where siphon cafés are still common.

How to Brew

Suggested ratio: 55–65g/litre
Grind size: Medium-fine
Buying advice: Siphons are, if I'm honest, unreasonably expensive. I probably wouldn't advocate for the largest size out there unless you have a specific need. Think carefully about how much you're really going to use this before you buy it. There's no question that it is one of the most theatrical brewers, but the delight of theatre diminishes with repeat viewings.

It is a tricky brewer and clean-up is slow and finicky (even with the papers). Speaking of which, I'd recommend buying a filter-paper adaptor unless you're already comfortable working and maintaining cloth for coffee brewing. They're a bit more work to align in the top chamber but do make the overall process much less painful.

STEP BY STEP

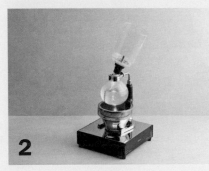

1 Grind the chosen amount of coffee just before brewing, but don't put it into the brewer yet.

Boil fresh, soft water in a kettle and then use it to fill the base of the siphon with your desired amount.

2 Make sure a clean filter is in place in the top chamber and then rest the top chamber in the base. Do not allow the bottom chamber to be sealed yet.

Using your chosen heat source, such as a small butane burner or specialized halogen heater, begin to heat the bottom chamber.

3 As the water comes to a boil, fully insert the top chamber.

When the water moves up to the top chamber, reduce the heat to low. Initially the bubbling will be quite vigorous, then it will lessen. Wait until this point and then look at the filter from directly above. If bubbles are coming from one side much more than the other, use a bamboo stirrer or long spoon to carefully push the filter into the middle.

4 Add the coffee.

Stir to properly wet all the grounds, and start a timer. After 30 seconds, gently stir the coffee again.

5 At 1 minute turn off the heat and then gently stir the coffee. I'd recommend stirring once clockwise and then once fully counter-clockwise. Or the other way round, it's up to you.

6 Once the coffee has drawn down completely, then remove the top chamber and decant all of the coffee. Beware – this is a very, very hot cup of coffee.

▸ Dialling It In

There are a few things to pay attention to with siphon brewing that make it one of the more challenging ways to get a great cup of coffee. The unusual aspects of the brew are the high, quite stable brew temperature during the infusion phase and then the negative pressure driving the percolation phase right at the end.

While this is primarily an infusion method, which means you could match your grind size to your steep time, I've struggled with longer brew times tasting harsh from the long duration at higher temperatures, so I tend to recommend a relatively short infusion.

Secondly, it is easy to have things go a little wrong during that final draw-down phase. You don't want to see a large dome at the end because this suggests uneven extraction. Ideally you don't want that final phase to stall either. Be gentle in your final stirs, and your grind might need a few small tweaks to get the best out of the coffee. Again, try and cool the coffee quickly if you can and don't try to assess it too hot – there'll be a bitterness and harshness that fades as it cools.

Finally, if you're using cloth, then do be dilligent about keeping it clean. Cafiza or any other organic espresso-machine cleaner will work well, but do rinse thoroughly afterwards.

Moka Pot

The Moka pot was created by Alfonso Bialetti's company in 1933, and very quickly became an iconic piece of design and a staple of Italian households, as well as homes around the world.

The Moka pot was invented to combine something of the new age of steam-powered espresso that was blossoming in Italy (high-pressure, modern-style espresso wouldn't appear until after 1948) with the three-piece design approach of the *napoletana*, a drip-style brewer that had a central part which held the coffee, gravity-dispersed water above it and a collection vessel below. Bialetti's company specialized in aluminium, and flipped the *napoletana*'s design on its head using steam to drive water up from the base, through the bed of coffee and into a collection chamber on the top, from which it was poured into a cup.

The coffee from a Moka pot is probably very close in style to early espresso – stronger than modern filter coffee, but not as intense as today's espresso. Used properly, these pots can produce delicious coffee, clean and sweet and well extracted.

Please clean your pot regularly (see page 127). The idea that a patina of dirt adds seasoning or any positives is not true – it will just add bitterness and harshness that will have you or your guests reaching for some sugar to help mask it.

How to Brew

Suggested ratio: 100g/litre
Grind size: Medium-fine
Buying advice: Bialetti Moka pots are the standard here. Typically their build quality is substantially better than other brands, meaning they not only look more pleasing but often fit together better too. This is a pressured vessel, so you want to be confident in the gaskets keeping the pressure in, and in the pressure-release valve that should let the pressure out safely should there be an issue.

People have lingering concerns about the safety of aluminium in these devices, though these appear unfounded. There is no evidence that shows any correlation between aluminium usage and Alzheimer's disease. However, I do prefer Bialetti's induction-suitable pots. I like their build quality more, they're heavier and I like the flexibility of being able to use them on a range of hobs. They are notably more expensive, but with proper care are products that should last a lifetime.

A note on sizes: Never fill the base of a Moka pot over the safety valve. This is because if the valve were to open it would eject pressurized hot water instead of steam. The fill level on a brew correlates to the basket holder too. Generally filling the water to the maximum level and filling the grounds holder without compressing it will give you a ratio of about 100g/litre. This ratio seems to hold across all brewers.

1 Make sure the pot is clean and that the rubber ring gaskets are clean and properly seated. Pay attention to the threading on both parts of the pot too, to make sure these are clean.

Add your coffee to the grounds holder. I don't recommend compressing the coffee, but make sure it is evenly distributed across the basket.

Boil a kettle, then fill the base with water just off the boil.

2 Gently drop the coffee holder into the base.

3 Using a towel to hold the base, screw the pot together. Make sure the rubber gasket is compressed and a good seal is formed.

4 Put the pot on to heat. The heat level should be medium-low. A high heat should not be used.

Leave the lid of the pot open.

Coffee should soon gently start to flow. At this point you want to reduce the heat as much as possible without stalling the flow of liquid. If using gas, then you need the lowest possible setting. With electric hobs you can often just turn it off and move the pot to the very edge.

Listen, if possible, to the brewer and when you hear sputtering and bubbling and hissing then it is time to remove from the heat. Alternatively, watch the stream of coffee and remove from the heat once you start to see the coffee spurting out and more steam leaving the brewer.

5 Run the base of the brewer under the cold tap. This stops the brewing process very quickly, preventing the brew temperature getting too high and the coffee becoming overly bitter.

Serve the coffee immediately. I would advise against leaving coffee inside the hot top part of the brewer, as this will degrade the flavour relatively quickly.

Drink and enjoy, but make sure to clean the brewer as soon as is convenient.

A note on cleaning: It is common to hear people talk positively about the patina that has formed on the inside of their brewer. This layer is dried liquid coffee, and I'm an advocate for removing this, or ideally preventing it forming. A cleaner brewer will produce less bitterness, though I understand that people's preference for bitterness does vary.

If a layer has formed, or you've found an old brewer and are trying to restore it, then I'd recommend soaking in espresso-machine cleaner (10g/litre of hot water). You may still need to give it a bit of a scrub and a second soak afterwards, depending on the state of the brewer, but it should eventually come away completely leaving you with a clean and happy Moka pot.

▶ Dialling It In

The trickiest part of a Moka pot can be dialling in both the grind and heat used. One of the reasons I like induction hobs is that you have an accurate and repeatable power setting, while gas can be harder to dial in accurately on many domestic stove pots. A little trial and error may be useful here. Go too low on the heat and your ground coffee can get very hot in the brewer, and that can cause some bitterness. Go too high and you may generate too much pressure in the brewer, leading to uneven brewing and harsh flavours.

Secondly, the grind size here is focused around making a strong coffee, without excess bitterness. You could grind finer and try and use less water for something closer in strength to an espresso, but at finer grind settings the window of good brewing does get smaller and the process more fussy and frustrating.

Finally, I should comment on the growing trend of using filter papers inside the brewer. You can put a filter paper in two places in a Moka pot: below the grounds or on top of the grounds, or both if you wish. They'll have different effects on brewing. A paper below the grounds will help with distribution of water going through the coffee cake. You can improve your brews a little this way, helping reduce uneven extraction. Most people use AeroPress filter papers for this. A paper on top of the grounds acts as an additional filter for the liquid coffee. It removes some of the oils and suspended pieces of ground coffee from the brew. You'll often see a little less foam, and there is some reduction in bitterness from this second level of filtration.

One quick check for dialling in the brew is to weigh the amount of coffee you get out. At most you can get about 65–70 per cent of the weight of water you put in. If you aren't getting this much out, and want more brewed liquid to help with extracting lighter roasts, then you need to reduce the heat further once liquid is flowing. If you're already at your lowest setting then you may need to move the pot on and off the heat, keeping an eye on the flow and using brief stints of heat if the flow slows, and allowing it to cool a little if the flow speeds up.

Automatic Coffee Maker

The automatic coffee maker has a few different names: a domestic coffee brewer, a batch brewer or a drip machine.

This brewer has been around for a long time now. Historically, most options were aimed at price and convenience over quality and performance. The first machine considered an automatic electric-drip coffee maker was probably the machine designed by Gottlob Widmann in 1954, called the Wigomat. The drip maker truly replaced the electric percolator with the rise in the US of the Mr Coffee brand in the 1970s.

The way that almost all makers work is that they have an element underneath the hotplate, and the brew water is heated by this and driven up a spout by its expansion and by steam, before being dispersed over the coffee.

How to Brew

Suggested ratio: 60g/litre
Grind size: Medium to medium-coarse
Buying advice: I'd advocate spending a bit more money on one of these if you can. Look for a unit certified by the Speciality Coffee Association (SCA) as being able to brew properly. With one of these brewers you can get great results, so then your decision is really down to style, price and features. I appreciate a machine that will brew at a certain time in the morning so I can wake to a freshly brewed pot. (The coffee could be better if it were freshly ground but 10 hours overnight isn't too damaging and I'm kinder in my assessment of the first cup of the day.)

I prefer thermal carafes for brewers because coffee sitting on a hot plate does start to taste off to me pretty quickly. Carafes do have downsides though - the coffee will lose heat a little quicker and they're a bit more work to clean. Often carafes don't pour as well, or as completely, as glass jugs, meaning some coffee is seemingly trapped inside - which is very annoying.

Maintenance: I'd recommend picking up some espresso-machine cleaner to help remove any staining that builds up inside the thermal carafe. I've long used Cafiza by Urnex, though other brands also work very well. The main concern, long term, with an automatic brewer is limescale formation. With any hardness at all in the water, this is inevitable and not really difficult to deal with. If you begin to notice the machine acting unusually - running too hot or too cold, or that the flow is slowing down - then it is time for a descale. You can easily pick up citric acid in many supermarkets or online, and it is a simple and food-safe descaler. Create a solution that is about 5 per cent citric acid and run it through the machine without putting coffee in the brew basket. Discard the liquid, and flush through another litre of water. If you want to be sure it is all gone, then brew a small amount of water and taste it. If it has a zingy acidity, then you need to keep flushing out the acid. This is completely food safe, so don't worry about ingesting citric acid like this.

Most of the cheap ones don't do a great job at hitting ideal temperatures. Initially the water is cooler than you might want and over the course of the brew it gets hotter and hotter, often ending up close to boiling. There are exceptions to this, but they are generally much more expensive. However, if you like the convenience of having a machine brew a large batch of coffee (I would say a need for more than 500ml of coffee would be a requirement for buying one), then they can be wonderful.

Domestic brewers don't really require a step-by-step guide. Put in the required amounts of coffee and soft water, press start and away you go. This automation and simplicity is part of the attraction. Instead, I'll give a few hacks and workarounds for various brewers that are perhaps cheaper, or aren't as feature-rich.

Temperature: Most cheaper machines brew at low temperatures. If you're brewing lighter roasts, then I'd recommend using hot water in the machine instead of cold. Nothing bad will happen, but the brew temperature will be much higher and the coffee much tastier. Heat the water in a kettle rather than using the hot tap in your sink.

The bloom: While some more expensive machines include a bloom phase, most do not. Blooming is beneficial and so there are a few different approaches. You can just pause the machine after it has started brewing a little bit. I'd pause for around 20–30 seconds, and be sure to swirl or stir the coffee too. Cheaper brewers often have a drip stop mechanism under the brew basket to prevent the last drips hitting the hotplate. This means that if you brew without the carafe in place the water will stay in the basket and you can have a kind of immersion phase bloom that works well too.

Stirring: Most machines benefit from a stir or swirl at the start and/or finish. However, the key sell of these machines is convenience, and so there has to be a balance between the pleasure of incrementally better coffee and the incrementally worse user experience.

▶ Dialling It In

Dialling in is a little frustrating here because of the amounts of coffee involved. I'd start with a medium grind, at the finer end for lighter roasts and the coarser end for darker roasts. Don't forget to stir the coffee in the carafe before tasting (though some carafes have a mixing funnel built in) and to let the coffee cool before tasting. If you taste it very hot, you'll often experience bitterness that fades a little, potentially tempting you to be coarser in your grind than you actually want.

5

ICED COFFEE AND COLD BREW

Depending where in the world you grew up, cold coffee can either seem like a wonderful, refreshing and uplifting salve for a hot day or something inexplicable, unappealing and bordering on inconceivable as a drink people might pay money for.

There are two approaches to cold coffee, and they each have ardent fans and are often pitted against each other. I'll look at both approaches, and discuss best practices for them, and I confess you'll probably find it pretty easy to work out which camp I'm in…

Iced Coffee

The defining difference between the two approaches is whether the coffee grounds are extracted with hot water or cold water. Firstly, I'll talk about brewing with hot water, and how this will impact your brewing process.

Iced Filter Coffee

You'll often see this style of brewing referred to as Japanese-style iced coffee. I'm not sure there's really sufficient evidence or precedent for this. Japan is also home to an astonishing myriad of canned cold coffee that is pretty unique. You'll also see this style of brewing labelled as flash-brewed iced coffee, which might seem a bit odd as it takes just as long as a normal pour-over, but in contrast to cold brew it is certainly far, far quicker.

As you're going to chill the coffee with ice, you need to compensate in some way for the dilution that will occur. A freshly brewed cup of filter coffee will need quite a weight of ice to chill it down sufficiently. The obvious adjustment is then to brew a stronger cup with less water, but as discussed on page 92 this makes proper extraction more difficult.

For chilling a pour-over-style brew, I've done a fair amount of testing and would say that about a third of your total brew water needs to be ice. So if you're brewing 30g of coffee and you'd usually use 500g of water for this, then you're going to use around 165–170g of ice and then brew the coffee with only 330–335g of water. You'll need to adjust your grind so it is a little bit finer, and you can also pour a little more slowly to try and increase the extraction a touch through a longer contact time.

As another option, the AeroPress is an excellent brewer for a single cup of iced coffee, as you can easily steep for longer before pressing on to ice. I've included recipes for both a small batch of iced pour-over coffee and a single-cup AeroPress overleaf.

Iced Pour-over

The base recipe is the same as the V60 technique on pages 104–5. However, you're going to make a few simple adjustments.

Firstly, 40 per cent of your brew water is going to be ice in the cup or carafe at the start of the brew. This means that for a 30g of coffee to 500g of water V60, here you'd be using 300g of water and 200g of ice.

As you're using less water, you're going to want to grind just a little bit finer. I'd also recommend increasing the ratio just a little bit – 65–70g of coffee per litre of water works well, to allow some additional dilution when you serve over ice.

Other than this you're going to follow the V60 recipe, though you'll obviously finish pouring the hot water earlier. Stir and swirl at the end to help an even extraction.

Most of the ice should have melted by the time you've finished brewing. If you find you have a lot of ice left over, reduce the amount next time and use a little more brew water to keep the overall amount of water used the same.

Iced AeroPress

The base recipe for this is the same as the AeroPress technique on pages 118–19. There are only a couple of adjustments to make.

Similarly to the iced V60 recipe given on the previous page, about 40 per cent of the overall brew water here is going to be ice in the cup or carafe.

With the AeroPress this means that you're either brewing quite a small brew or brewing for two – a rare occasion when the AeroPress is able to make coffee for more than just one person.

For one cup it would be 12g of coffee, 120g of hot water, brewing on to 80g of ice. For two cups, it would 24g of coffee, 240g of water and 160g of ice. The limit of an AeroPress is about 240g of water.

Increasing the steep time here is helpful, so I'd recommend adding 2 minutes to the main steep time given in the recipe on pages 118–19.

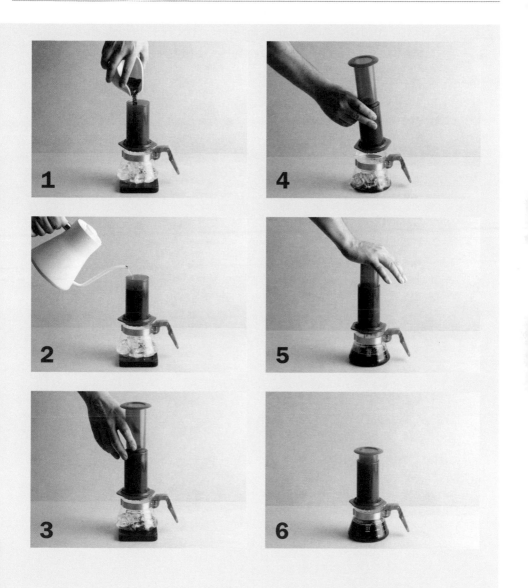

Iced Espresso Drinks

The other category of iced coffee drinks that are brewed hot are espresso-based drinks, such as iced americanos or iced lattes.

Historically, iced espresso was frowned upon because the process of chilling the espresso and slightly diluting it really intensified the perceived bitterness of the resulting cup. You'd often hear of people or cafés refusing to serve it because the ice 'shocked' the espresso. This language is, in my opinion, a little questionable. Colder espresso has a higher level of perceived bitterness, regardless of whether or not you do it quickly or slowly. Diluting an espresso also increases the perceived bitterness, as it does in an americano too.

Due to the increased bitterness of iced espresso drinks, it is pretty common to see most iced versions sweetened a little bit to compensate for this. It is by no means necessary, but it is good to understand why many iced lattes are served a bit sweeter.

In terms of technique, there's very little to adjust or change when making iced espresso drinks – other than to consider that your serving vessel will need to be a little bigger to hold the additional ice as well as the diluted and chilled finished beverage.

For more espresso recipes, see pages 204–13.

Cold Brew Coffee

Brewing coffee with cold or room temperature water is surprisingly polarizing. For some it is the only way they feel they can drink coffee, for others it is undrinkable and stale. Before I get into why it is so divisive, let's look at brewing theory to understand what makes cold brew different.

As discussed on page 94, the hotter brewing water gets, the more efficient and effective it is when it comes to extracting soluble flavours from ground coffee. At cooler temperatures it doesn't extract some acids and other compounds, and as a result produces a cup that people enjoy for being low in acidity, and that's often purported to cause less digestive issues, such as acid reflux. The lower brew temperature also has a big impact on the flavour of the cup. Many people enjoy the more chocolatey and round flavour profiles of cold brew.

There are challenges with cold brewing. Firstly, because the water is cooler and less effective at extracting flavour it takes longer for an infusion brew to properly extract. This problem is compounded by the fact that you can't just quickly compensate by grinding the coffee much finer – which seems the obvious solution. Filtering finely ground coffee from cold water is quite difficult, and this means that brewing is typically done with a coarser grind than you might for a pour-over. This means that the solution to cold brewing effectively is usually to brew for long

periods of time. This does work quite well, but unfortunately it gives the brewing liquid plenty of time to interact with the oxygen in the environment, which gives a lot of cold-brewed coffee an oxidized taste that many people find deeply unpleasant. However, to others it is just 'cold brew flavour' and not only pleasant but desirable. I can't present my own subjective preferences as objective fact, so I would never say cold brew is inferior.

One additional challenge is that to compensate for lower extractions, even over long times, from coarsely ground coffee it is common to see high coffee-to-water ratios used. This increase produces a stronger cup of coffee, though it is difficult for it to be properly extracted. However, because you're brewing with cold water the taste of underextraction is really quite different. Usually underextracted coffee tastes sour and acidic. The acids which produce that taste seem to need hotter water to extract, so an underextracted cold brew is often only overtly unpleasant if it is weak as well. Higher coffee-to-water ratios have two main downsides, though some might argue one of them. Firstly, the cost per cup is notably higher and in part this is because you're leaving some good flavours in the spent coffee grounds, which is wasteful. The other potential issue is that caffeine is pretty water soluble, so cold brew often seems to come with a more significant kick of caffeine. For some that's good news, for others it really, really isn't. There is, of course, no good reason that cold brew couldn't be made from decaf, or half-caf, and be tasty and enjoyable.

There are a number of brewers and gadgets entering the market, promising to produce a faster cup of cold brew. They might use agitation, or pressure, or other means to increase the rate of extraction. They allow you to use less coffee, have a shorter brew time and potentially avoid some of the oxidation flavours if you don't like those. There isn't space here to dive into a review of each and every unit, so this isn't something I can cover in this book. My experience so far has left me sceptical but hopeful – it should be possible to produce quick, efficient cold brew this way. However, you'll never have a cup that resembles hot coffee or iced brewed coffee. There's no way to cheat temperature.

I've gone backward and forward on whether or not to include a cold brew recipe here. I've chosen not to because to date I don't feel like I've come up with a new variation on existing techniques that I particularly like and reproducing other people's recipes here seems contrary to the idea of this book. If you enjoy cold brew, then I'd encourage experimentation as it is probably the most tolerant method of brewing coffee. You can miss the grind size a little, you can brew for more or less hours than intended (26 hours of brewing when aiming for 24 is barely noticeable) and still get close to something you will enjoy – and that is no bad thing.

HOW TO MAKE GREAT ESPRESSO

Espresso can be a glorious thing. Intense, rich, complex but also fleeting. It has, over the last few decades, managed to ascend to the point that many people see as the pinnacle of coffee. I'm not one of those people, but I absolutely understand the allure and enjoyment of this fascinating brew method.

Making yourself a truly excellent espresso is an incredibly satisfying achievement, but it would be irresponsible of me not to highlight the time, energy and resources that getting to that point can take. A lot of people ask me whether they should buy an espresso machine: after all, they enjoy an espresso or a cappuccino and the idea of having this on tap in the home is very tempting. My answer is always a question: 'Do you want a new hobby?' Not everyone does, and many people are surprised that I don't have an espresso machine at home either.

In this chapter I'll discuss the wide range of variables and aspects of espresso brewing, from equipment to technique. I want people to enjoy coffee above all else, and so it is perfectly fine if that coffee comes from a great café who is willing to invest in great equipment, great coffee, in training and also in the cleaning up afterwards that comes with it all!

The Principles of Espresso

Espresso was created to solve a problem: to brew quickly you need to grind your coffee finely so you can extract all the flavour in a limited window. The problem, when you grind this finely, is that gravity alone won't get the brew water through the bed of coffee.

In order to drive water through the ground coffee, and to make sure your brew still happens quickly, you need pressure. Initially this pressure came from steam trapped inside a boiler, and it wasn't that high – it was maybe 1–2 bars of pressure. The resulting drink wasn't an intense shot of coffee topped with a golden-brown layer of crema. At its inception, espresso was much closer to Moka-pot brewing or even filter coffee. Innovations and improvements mean that we can now use electric pumps, or compressed springs or just the power of our arms through levers, to create much higher pressures to make espresso as we know it today.

The name 'espresso' comes from the same word having two meanings in Italian, in the same way as 'express' does in English. It means both 'fast' and also 'pressed out'. Its speed, and its flexibility as an ingredient, make it popular in businesses as a way to serve a lot of different coffee drinks to a lot of different people. However, the fact that espresso is often the first and only choice for coffee making in many businesses, and perhaps enhanced by the world's love affair with aspects of Italian culture, means that espresso has taken the top spot in many people's perception of coffee as the 'best' way to make coffee – the pinnacle of coffee brewing.

This is not true. Espresso is a wonderful way to make coffee but it doesn't make better coffee than any other method. In fact, the intensity of espresso preparation – the short brew times, high brewing pressures and finely ground coffee – all come together to make for a tricky, often frustrating way to make coffee. It has been argued that espresso is the fussiest, most difficult preparation in the entire culinary world and, to be honest, I'm not sure that I can effectively disagree.

However, once you understand the key principles of espresso you can effectively control them. While absolute perfection will likely remain elusive, I think it is perfectly possible to easily and repeatedly make very enjoyable espresso every day.

Espresso is About Creating Resistance

A good espresso machine will push hot water forward at a repeatable pressure and temperature. To control how the espresso brews, you are controlling how easy or how

difficult it is for the water to pass through the coffee. The slower the water passes through, the more flavour it is likely to extract. This seems relatively simple, but where espresso sneaks up on you and frustrates you is that very small changes to your recipe or preparation can completely change the resulting taste of your espresso.

Primarily you can control resistance with two variables: the amount of coffee in the basket and the grind size of the coffee. It is fairly obvious that having more coffee in the basket will create more resistance and a slower brew. I'll discuss it again later, but it is worth pointing out that very small changes – half a gram of coffee – can have a very noticeable impact on how the espresso brews.

It is best to think about grind size in terms of sand or pebbles. If you tried to build a dam out of pebbles, the water would easily find a way through the gaps between the pieces, but if you use sand then you'll create more resistance because the gaps get much smaller. The same is true with coffee: a finer grind creates more resistance and a slower brew.

The way we tend to measure espresso is with two other variables: the amount of liquid pushed through the bed of coffee, and the time it took. This allows you to measure the flow rate but also control the recipe and understand

what changes you need to make to have the coffee taste better or keep it tasting good.

Of these four variables (amount of coffee, grind size, amount of liquid espresso and brew time), you'll often see three of them presented as part of a recipe. A roaster might recommend using 18g of ground coffee to produce 36g of liquid espresso in around 28–30 seconds. It would be helpful if they could somehow tell you what grind size to use, but we have no effective way of communicating grind size. The only way you can find the right grind size is to brew the recipe of weight in and out, and see how long the brew takes. Then adjust your grind until you get your desired brew time.

This process is called 'dialling in' within the coffee industry, and wider community. It can, initially, feel like a process of trial and error and there are a few common mistakes that people make which can make the whole process seem chaotic or counter-intuitive. I'll cover these over the next few pages.

Channelling

A complicating factor in espresso is that the very high pressures you're working with can cause issues. You need higher pressure in order to get water through the dense bed of finely ground coffee, but under pressure water is looking for the path of least resistance. In order to have truly delicious espresso you want the water to pass very evenly through the bed of coffee. However, what can easily happen is that water finds a less dense pocket of coffee and begins to flow quickly through it. This is called channelling.

When espresso channels, a higher percentage of water passes through a small section of the coffee bed. This small pocket of coffee will have its flavour extracted much more effectively, often to the point that it begins to give up harsh, very bitter tastes. This then leaves comparatively less water for the rest of the coffee, so that coffee isn't properly extracted and contributes sourness to the final cup. A badly channelled espresso brew tastes pretty awful.

Our understanding of channelling, what causes it, how to prevent it and just how common it is, has evolved dramatically over the last few years. A word of warning: even the most practised barista, using every tool available to them, will still have channelling in their shots sometimes. Ideally, just not very much. Under such high water pressures it is incredibly difficult to avoid some channelling, but when brewing espresso your focus on preparing an even coffee bed will be rewarded by more delicious shots. I'll cover puck preparation techniques and tamping on pages 186–9.

I'll note now that brew temperature is also often discussed and frequently included in espresso recipes supplied by coffee roasters or in online communities. Many machines can now control the brew temperature easily, using digital controls on the user interface. I'll discuss it in more detail, but when trying to understand the key principles of dialling in I wanted to keep it separate.

Over the next few pages I'll talk about the practical process of dialling in and about how you might tune your recipe or technique for the coffee you are working with. A number of factors can influence the way a coffee brews and tastes as espresso. You're always going to be chasing the best-tasting espresso, and taste will lead the way and guide your decisions.

Dialling In Espresso By Taste
With a little practice you can use the taste of your espresso to guide you toward changing the right variable, making the right tweak and being more successful with your next brew. Many people feel intimidated or frustrated by the idea of using taste as they feel they lack the experience or skills of a professional taster.

When people talk about coffee extraction you'll hear the phrases underextraction and overextraction used a lot. For a fuller explanation of those terms, then make sure you've revisited The Universal Theory of

Coffee Brewing on pages 88–9. I'm going to be looking at two key elements of taste that correlate to different flaws in your extraction: acidity and bitterness.

Acidity is present in most speciality coffee, though the level will vary with roast level, variety, process or the terroir of the farm. Acidity is a wonderful aspect to the taste experience, in coffee and across the entire culinary world. The challenge with acidity is, for many people, it can be a tricky one to balance. A dominant and unpleasant acidity is never really enjoyable. A crisp, green apple has a delightfully intense acidity, but straight lime juice is less fun. The level of acidity you enjoy in coffee is particular to you, and part of the journey is finding out what kind of coffees you enjoy and how you like to brew them. However, you can use acidity as a very clear indicator of the level of extraction you have.

If you underextract a coffee, it will likely have a dominant and unpleasant acidity. This is down to acidic compounds in coffee being highly soluble. As you extract more and more from the coffee, you balance out that acidity and the drink becomes increasingly pleasant. There is, of course, a point that you cross where extracting too much from the coffee begins to taint the experience and this comes in the form of intense, lingering and unpleasant bitterness.

BITTER SOUR CONFUSION

Bitter sour confusion is a commonly experienced phenomenon, where unpleasant and harsh acidity is confused with bitterness. This is particularly unhelpful in coffee where they could indicate opposing problems! You'll occasionally still see tongue maps, showing where you taste acidity or salt. These are a confusing representation – your taste buds are all over your tongue and they detect all the tastes across them. However, many people experience acidity down the sides of their tongue, and it is immediate on tasting a coffee. Bitterness tends to be experienced across the tongue and down into the throat, and in coffee can increase in intensity after swallowing. If you're looking for a practical example, the next time you make a salad dressing is the perfect opportunity to experience some pure acidity (in the form of vinegar or lemon juice) as well as bitterness (if you're using a good-quality olive oil).

If you brew an espresso and find the acidity is too much, and the body/texture of the espresso is a little weak/thin, then you can be confident that you need to extract more from the coffee. Most likely your grind is too coarse, and the contact time between the water and coffee was too fast. There are other ways you can change the extraction, and I'll discuss the variables of brewing espresso next, but the balance of acidity is really the primary driver behind the decisions you'll make and the variables you'll choose to change.

Recipes and Ratios

The modern style of espresso brewing is often described and communicated in terms of both recipes and ratios.

Historically, the size of the liquid espresso was communicated in ml, but that is falling increasingly out of favour. The challenge with communicating the size of an espresso by volume is that a portion of that volume in espresso is crema. Crema is a foam of the liquid espresso, created when CO_2 comes out of solution and gets trapped by the foaming agents in the coffee. The amount of crema you get in an espresso correlates pretty strongly to the amount of CO_2 trapped in the coffee grounds when you brew them. This means that fresher coffee produces more crema, and there are other variables too such as roast level or whether you are brewing pure arabica or some robusta too. As such, if you made a 30ml espresso with very fresh coffee, then a larger percentage of that volume would be trapped gasses, and the same volume of an older coffee would have had more water pushed through the grounds to make up for the missing gas volume to get the total volume up to 30ml. So what might look identical in terms of output in the brewing time would actually be dramatically different, and they would taste pretty different too. The move to weighing the liquid espresso has helped remove this variable because the gas has little to no measurable impact on the weight of the liquid espresso. Your 40g of liquid espresso will have a larger volume if made from fresher coffee, but you'd have extracted it very similarly to a matching recipe of an older coffee.

Crema

Crema is one of the definitive qualities of espresso, and there is a great deal of romance around it. It unquestionably makes the drink appear more appetizing but the goal should always be the best-tasting espresso, not the best-looking one. As mentioned opposite, crema is formed from CO_2 being trapped as bubbles in the espresso, making it a reasonably stable foam. When water is under high pressures, as it is during espresso brewing, then it is able to dissolve more CO_2 than normal, becoming 'supersaturated' with CO_2. As the espresso exits the brewing basket in the portafilter, the liquid returns to normal atmospheric pressure and the CO_2 comes out of the solution as bubbles.

Crema seems to trap little particles of ground coffee that have made it through the basket, often creating a pleasing pattern on top of the crema that is known as 'tiger stripes'. Darker roasts tend to produce these more, and they do make the espresso a feast for the eyes. Crema is often seen as a maker or indicator of quality, and to a limited degree that is true. Badly brewed espresso, or espresso brewed from stale coffee, will not produce any lasting crema, so an absence of crema is certainly a red flag for what you're about to drink (assuming you've been served the espresso quickly, as crema does dissipate quite rapidly). However, low-quality, fresh-roasted coffee, brewed in a dirty machine, will produce plenty of crema and you'll get a pretty terrible espresso at the end of it, so don't place too much faith in the dense brown foam on the top of your coffee.

Hopefully it now makes sense why you want to pay attention to the weight of the liquid espresso you're brewing, rather than its volume, if you're trying to control your espresso brewing properly. The cost of a cheap set of small digital scales is very quickly offset by the massive reduction in coffee wasted chasing a better-tasting espresso by eye. Before I proceed with the rest of the recipe factors, I want to touch on ratios in espresso brewing.

Ratios

You'll see a lot of discussion about ratios in espresso communities, online or in the real

world. It refers to the ratio of ground coffee to liquid espresso. If you took 18g of coffee and brewed 36g of liquid, then you'd have a 1:2 ratio. There are a couple of ideas around ratios that are important. The first is why ratios are helpful across so many culinary areas (baking in particular). If you increase the amount of one component, then you should maintain your ratio and this helps you calculate how much of the other component you might need. If you change your coffee dose to 20g, then you need to increase the amount of liquid you push through the coffee to 40g.

What gets confusing, but is really important, is that if you brew two different recipes, and extract them in the same brew time and at the same brew temperature, then the espresso from an 18g in and 36g out should taste identical to an espresso made from 20g in and 40g out. There'd just be more of it to drink from the latter brew. In the real world this is very rarely the case, and some of why is touched upon on pages 148–53 where I discuss espresso brewing theory. So while fixed ratios are not the solution to every problem, you should be making sure you keep them relatively constant if you're making small changes to how you brew your espresso.

The second area in which ratios have become quite useful is offering up some definitions for different espresso variations. Historically there were really three interpretations of espresso: ristretto, espresso and the lungo. As straight translations, 'ristretto' means a restricted espresso and 'lungo' means a long espresso. Now we can use ratios as a way defining these drinks, though these are very much guidelines more than absolutes.

A ristretto is often described as anything from 1:1 to 1:1.5. You could have a more intense ratio than 1:1 but the chances of properly extracting the coffee and having it taste good are slim to none. An espresso can now be defined as anything from 1:1.5 to 1:3. A lungo would then be any ratio greater than 1:3, though above 1:6 or 1:7 it is getting close to being a filter coffee made with an espresso machine.

If someone is coming to espresso brewing for the first time, then I'd generally recommend a 1:2 ratio for any coffee that has been specifically roasted to be brewed as espresso. This isn't a one size fits all, but generally you'll be close to where you need to be and able to make a few simple adjustments to tweak the way the espresso brews to fix aspects of its taste that aren't quite right.

Understanding ratios in espresso is helpful for both communicating and understanding recipes shared by roasters or online, and also for understanding the base idea of a recipe and controlling key variables to help you make something delicious more often.

How to Adjust a Grinder

The area that generates the most frustration in making espresso for those fairly early on in their journey down the coffee rabbit-hole is adjusting the grinder.

The principle seems so simple – if you want to slow down the flow of water through the coffee, and extract more flavour from your grinds, then a finer grind is what is needed. Similarly, to speed up the flow of water through the coffee, you'd want to grind the coffee coarser.

There are two main reasons that people find themselves stuck in a loop where the coffee doesn't do what they want it to do. The first is caused by retention inside the grinder. Almost every grinder will retain a small amount of coffee, and many retain a significant amount between the burrs and exit chute where the coffee comes out. This means that when you adjust the grinder and grind your next dose, the coffee you are getting is a mixture of the previous grind setting and the new grind setting. This is a problem. Let's say you wanted to grind finer, and you brew this mixture of grinds. The flow will be slower, but may not be slow enough. If you immediately change the grind setting again, then your next brew will still be a mixture of grind sizes. The solution is simple, but also frustrating. The best practice is to purge the grinder – to grind a small amount of coffee to push out the old grind size and then to throw this away. This is wasteful, annoying, the result of bad design and also a bit of a variable. In many modern single-dose grinders the amount might only be 5g. In many commercial espresso grinders you need to purge 20g+ of coffee, which can be very bad for business. However, it is better to purge 5g of coffee than to grind 18g without purging and have a terrible espresso as a result.

The second area that frustrates people is knowing how much to adjust a grinder by. How far should you turn the collar or dial toward finer or coarser? It is hard to give absolute rules here, but with a stepped grinder a change of one step will typically change the brew time by around 3–4 seconds for a fixed ratio. With a stepless grinder it is normal

to have some sort of indication, be it lines, notches or other markers, and each marker typically makes a similar sized adjustment. While there are exceptions, I'd generally avoid making very large adjustments unless your brewing is a long, long way from normal or good.

Brew Temperatures and Pump Pressures

Both of these variables have generated a great deal of discussion in the last couple of decades of espresso brewing.

In part because the impact of these has been understood with more nuance, and in part because the coffee community demanded things that were relatively simple technical problems for manufacturers to solve, and so they did so with much fanfare that in turn increased the volume of conversation around that particular variable.

Brew Temperatures

The classic example of this is brew temperature. In the early 2000s, a small number of professionals and enthusiastic home baristas began experimenting with trying to control brew temperature in their espresso machine more precisely. Up until this point machines had been reasonably, but not absolutely, consistent in their brewing temperature. Manufacturers were initially slow to respond to the new demands for flatline temperatures, as if it were an admission of a flaw in their existing models, but slowly and surely they all found ways of having their machines produce a fixed and consistent temperature during the brew.

This technology also arrived at a time before people understood espresso extraction fully, and before people were weighing their shots.

This lead many people to believe that very small changes in temperature, less than 0.5°C (1°F), were having significant impact on the espresso's taste. It now seems more likely that they were brewing pretty variable shots due to going by eye, and while the hotter shot might have been better, the small bump in temperature may not have been why.

This is not to say brew temperature is not worthy of discussion. Brew temperature has an impact on taste, and having a machine be able to deliver consistent brew temperatures is helpful. (Though I will say that the number of bad espressos in my life which could have been fixed by a small change in brew temperature alone is a fraction of a per cent of the bad espressos I've drunk.)

Increasing brew temperature will help increase your extraction, and often decrease acidity and increase sweetness, but only to a point. It won't overcome fundamental flaws in your ratio, recipe, brew time or grind size. It is a nice little tweak when something is very close to excellent, to help get a little bit more.

It is important to vary the brew temperature according to the roast degree of the coffee you are brewing. Light roasts can tolerate and benefit from higher temperatures because they have less of the bitter compounds that are very soluble at higher temperatures. Brew temperatures of 92–97°C (198–207°F) for lighter roasts are appropriate. For medium roasts, I'd start somewhere between 88°C (190°F) and 94°C (201°F), going cooler for the darker end of the spectrum. For dark roasts, I'd be brewing between 80°C (176°F) and 85°C (185°F) to minimize bitterness, unless you particularly enjoy that kind of bitterness and then you can certainly brew hotter.

However, I'm hesitant to talk in absolutes about brew temperature because it further compounds the idea that flatline temperature brewing is somehow better or ideal. The truth is that we don't know that for sure yet. What we do know are important are repeatability and control. However, there are many machines that produce a profile of temperature during the brew due to the nature of their technology. These machines are perfectly capable of producing delicious espresso.

We're also on the cusp of seeing reliable temperature-profiling in espresso machines, where you're able to adjust the temperature during the course of the brew. This is interesting, but we're a long way from knowing what to do with it. Which leads us neatly into the second part of this section.

Pump Pressures

Espresso is defined as being brewed under relatively high pressures, but there's a lot of confusion around the topic. The most commonly recommended pressure you'll see is 9 bars. However, to understand this and properly replicate or achieve it, you need to understand the nature of pressure creation and control in most espresso machines.

In commercial espresso machines, with rotary pumps, it is common to see a pressure gauge that goes to 9 bars when the pump is activated and coffee is in the handle. This pressure is being measured very close to the pump and represents that maximum pressure in the system. If you flush the group head of a coffee machine, to rinse off the coffee from the screen from the previous brew, then you'll notice that the water doesn't seem to be flowing out under any pressure, despite very high pressures showing on the gauge. This is because the pressure is not constant throughout the system and without any resistance there is a decline in pressure between the pump and the group head. When you put coffee in the handle, then there is some resistance and the full force of the pump is able to be exerted on to the coffee. However, when people began to measure the pressure at the group head with tools designed to replicate an espresso puck they saw that the pressure was only 8 bars. This is because it isn't a sealed system, and just as in espresso brewing, pressure is escaping as the liquid flows through the coffee puck and out into the cup. The resistance you create in the puck will determine how much of the pressure the machine created gets to the coffee. Very coarsely ground coffee would be brewing under relatively low pressures, and very finely ground coffee would get pretty close to 9 bars as the liquid barely made its way through.

With machines that use vibration pumps it is common to have the pump running at higher pressures than 9 bars, and then to use an over pressure valve (OPV) to bleed off any pressure above 9 bars. Sadly, most domestic machines do not have their OPV set correctly and although fixing it is not difficult, it does involve opening an electrical appliance and making modifications – which may void warranties, and is dangerous if you don't know what you're doing with electrical appliances. So I would not broadly recommend it.

Before 1961 it was very common for espresso machines to use spring levers to generate the necessary pressure for brewing. These did not produce a fixed pressure; instead they produced their maximum pressure just after they were released at the start of the brew. This pressure would decline during the brew, as the spring expanded and had less elastic potential energy. Electric pumps gained popularity with the success of FAEMA's E61 machine in 1961, which used a rotary pump.

This also perhaps represents the moment of creation of a split in the espresso community – those who like flat pressures, and those who like pressure curves, or profiles.

Pressure was not the subject of a great deal of interest or experimentation in the wider coffee community until La Marzocco released their Strada machines, which allow pre-programmed pressure profiles to be executed by the machine using gear pumps. This technology, and the idea of pressure profiling, initially generated a lot of interest and excitement but it has taken perhaps a decade of experimentation from a variety of manufacturers in order for there to be some understanding about the potential benefits of pressure profiling in espresso brewing.

In order to discuss pressure profiles in espresso, I need to talk about the first moments of espresso brewing, usually described as pre-infusion.

The Pre-infusion Phase
This term has been around for quite a long time, but discussion about it has intensified in the era of modern coffee brewing. In almost every espresso machine, the first seconds of the brew do not happen under full pressure. This is because initially the water is soaking into the coffee, and filling the space above the coffee inside the brewing chamber. Until the whole chamber is completely full of water,

the full force of the pump pressure being generated isn't able to be translated to the coffee. Some machines slow this down further by forcing the water through a very small hole (usually around 0.5mm in diameter, though it varies), which slows the flow rate and the rate at which the system reaches full pressure. This is why it usually takes 6–10 seconds after you hit the button on the machine for coffee to appear.

What gets more confusing is that this term represents a *phase* of espresso brewing, but also a *goal* of espresso brewing. The goal is to make sure that the entire puck of ground coffee has become wet before the full force from the pump begins to exert its pressure. There are a number of potential explanations as to why this might be the case, but I can say with some certainty that having pre-infusion properly achieved helps with the evenness of the extraction during the brew, which improves the flavour of the espresso.

In many machines it is possible to extend or control the pre-infusion in some ways, and generally speaking I would recommend experimenting with this to find the point at which the puck is wet but not yet under full pressure. This is easiest with a naked portafilter, one which has been modified to expose the bottom of the brewing basket usually hidden inside. I'd recommend adding one of these to your collection if you want to

improve your espresso-brewing technique. (For more on portafilter components see pages 166–7.)

The one method that I wouldn't recommend is where the machine turns on the pump for a bit, turns it off, waits, then turns it on again. In theory this should add a pre-infusion phase, but often this process is just very disruptive. If any pressure at all has built up inside the brew chamber it is discharged back through the group head, causing a brief upward force on the puck, which can break it apart a bit. So when the pump does then come back on at full force, there are likely to be gaps in the puck that will cause channelling.

The Main Brewing Phase
Modifying pressure during the rest of the brewing phase of an espresso is worth exploring, though this can easily lead you down a road where every shot tastes a little different – but nothing tastes better and most taste worse than with no pressure profiling. Which can be frustrating, to say the very least. It is still very much an active area of exploration within both professional and domestic espresso communities.

The best guidance I can offer is to pay attention to flow. The flow rate is defined as the speed at which water is moving through the puck of coffee. Pressure and flow have a relationship – it would make sense that the higher the pressure, the faster the water would be pushed through the coffee. However, this isn't always true. Pressures above 9 bars can compress the puck of coffee so much that the flow rate actually starts to drop again. Some people have speculated that 9 bars was chosen as the preferred brew pressure because it yielded the highest flow in the bell curve of pressure and flow.

What is interesting about watching flow is that it can tell you a lot about espresso. A constant pressure from a pump does not yield a constant flow in an espresso brew. During the second half of the shot the flow will begin to increase, getting faster and faster. This is because the espresso-brewing process is eroding and dissolving the puck of coffee. There is less coffee there at the end of an espresso than at the start.

There is an argument that reducing the pump pressure during the shot is helpful to maintain a steady flow rate. This is something that lever machines do (see pages 168–70), and may be one of the reasons many people like the espresso from them. What may be another benefit of reducing pressure during the shot is that you are less likely to open and exploit new channels in the coffee bed due to the water being under such high pressure. The further into an espresso brew you get, the more likely you are to see channelling, and a pressure reduction here may be the easiest way to mitigate this issue, if your machine will let you do it.

The final guidance I will give is that 9 bars is no longer considered the gold standard. You can achieve excellent espressos at lower pressures. If you have an entry- to mid-level espresso grinder, then brewing at something like 6 bars may be a great way to improve the evenness of your extraction and it will also be kinder to your technique if you're still developing your skills around puck prep (the process of dosing, distributing and tamping the coffee before brewing, see pages 184–7).

Portafilter Components

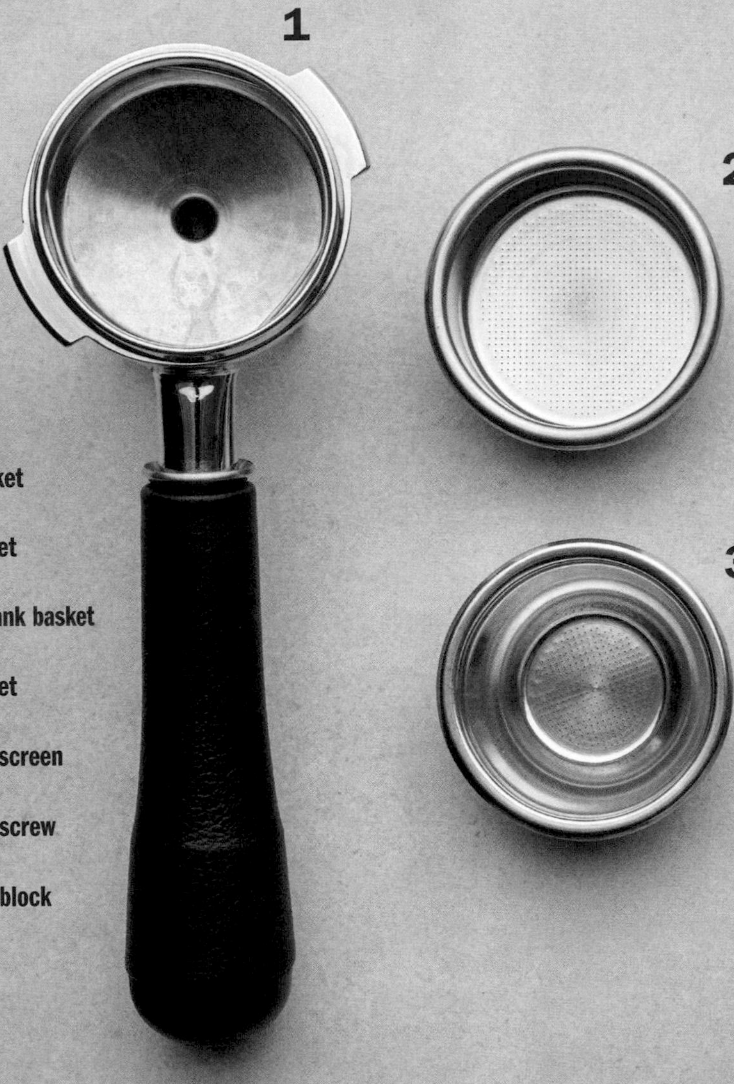

1

2

3

1. Portafilter

2. Double basket

3. Single basket

4. Cleaning blank basket

5. Group gasket

6. Dispersion screen

7. Dispersion screw

8. Dispersion block

4

6

7

5

8

How to Buy an Espresso Machine

An espresso machine is, for most people, the single most expensive coffee-related purchase they'll make.

An espresso machine holds the promise of such pleasure, of intense and delightful coffee experiences at a fraction of the cost of a café, at a time and place of your convenience. The truth of it is that espresso is unquestionably a hobby, and one that most people don't actually want. Making espresso is time-consuming, messy and all too easily it is deeply, profoundly frustrating. For someone who is passionate about coffee to talk about it in such a negative way seems odd, but it is important to me that if you're going to spend a ton of money on a piece of coffee equipment, then you should enjoy using it. If the idea of the end drink is more appealing than dialling in espresso each morning, then I'd honestly recommend a different brew method for home and to treat yourself to espresso drinks from a great café (if you have one near you, which I know is far from everyone).

An espresso machine, at it's basic level, does a relatively simple thing: it uses high pressures to push hot water through a bed of finely ground coffee. This simple requirement is met reasonably well by almost every espresso machine no matter its price point. This can make trying to choose a new machine, and understanding what you really get for your money, difficult. The approach of this section is to break apart a few aspects of how a machine works and to look at the varying options available and their cost implications. This should then help you to break down the feature list of a machine you're considering and help you understand whether or not it is going to meet your needs.

How a Machine Creates High Pressure

Pressure is important to espresso brewing; you can see more about its impact in the section on Pump Pressures, pages 162–3. There are four main ways a machine can create the necessary pressures for espresso brewing (around 9 bars or 130psi). Let's explore them.

1. Manual Machines

These are machines that have no internal components for creating pressure; instead they use a system where the pressure comes from you, the barista. Most commonly these are lever machines, where you push down on a lever to create the requisite amount of pressure. Better machines will have gauges showing you how much pressure you've created because the primary challenge of these machines, aside from being a brief morning workout, is consistency. Consistency of pressure is difficult to achieve with a lever machine, and that can be frustrating when

it comes to repeatability. Small variances are unlikely to turn a good shot into an awful one, but you will find that reproducing something truly astonishing is difficult and you'll benefit from a little practice.

There are other systems that don't use direct levers, that use some other method of converting your work into brewing pressure, but without the physics of levers these can be very hard work. The upside of manual machines is that not having a pump of any kind does make them comparatively cheaper. An additional benefit is the tactile aspect of brewing this way, though this isn't universal. It gives you unlimited control of the process, for better or worse. There's undoubtedly a feeling of connection and craft in using a lever, and for many people this makes the process of making espresso ritualistic, and perhaps more intimate. Be aware that the fun can wear off, and you might soon wish to outsource this part of the process to something more repeatable and less physical.

2. Spring Lever Machines

These kinds of lever machine can initially look like manual lever machines but they have one key difference. Inside the group head, above the piston that drives water through the coffee, is a large spring. Pulling down the lever compresses the spring, and releasing the lever allows the spring to expand, pressing the water through the coffee as it does. The first true espresso machine, that reached high brewing pressures, worked this way.

The benefits of a spring lever are two-fold: firstly it is a consistent way to make coffee. The spring expands in a predictable and repeatable way, meaning that shot to shot you'll have little variance coming from this part of the process. Secondly, as the spring expands, the force it exerts begins to drop. This produces a simple pressure profile where the pressure might spike as high as 12 bars initially and drop down to 3 or 4 over the course of the brew. (It doesn't drop lower than this before the chamber holding the spring prevents it expanding further, so it is always under some tension.)

Like a manual-lever machine, this has a cost benefit where the cost of the technology doesn't really impact the price of the machine heavily. However, like a manual machine, there is still some work to do. You have to pull hard to compress the spring, and that is quite physical and demanding for many people. In addition, there is a small risk of letting go of the lever before it is fully pulled down (there's usually a locking mechanism at the bottom). If you release it before the chamber has filled with water properly, or without any resistance in the way when flushing ground coffee off the shower screen, then the lever can whip back up at great speed and with great force, with the lever typically travelling in an arc near the barista's face. There have been many reports over the years of painful and unpleasant accidents. Being mindful of this when using it is important. These machines can be used very safely very easily, but it is worth bearing in mind.

3. Vibration Pumps

When it comes to generating high pressures through electrical components, then the cheapest and most common way to do this is with a vibration pump. These are small and cheap, and capable of producing higher pressures than are needed in espresso brewing. This particular aspect is why they can also be frustrating for a consumer.

If you look on the boxes for many domestic espresso machines, you'll see various claims about the machine being able to produce 15 bars of pressure or more. In a scenario where you want only 9 bars, this isn't actually good news. The technology that better machines use to moderate the pressure is called an over pressure valve (OPV). These are small mechanical valves designed to release excess pressure in a system as a way of controlling the pressure sent to the coffee. A vibration pump might produce 12 bars, but if you set the over pressure valve to 9 bars, then any additional pressure that is built up is typically released and sent back to the water tank. However, these are rarely set correctly from factory for a few reasons. It might be

that the manufacturer doesn't see this as important, it might be that the machine is designed expecting the end consumer to be putting pre-ground, coarsely ground coffee into it. In this scenario the results would usually be terrible, but in combination with specific baskets that restrict the pressure inside, the results can be improved to the point of being average, but not awful.

If you're looking to get the best out of a machine with a vibration pump, then it is worth reading more about how other users have found it to be set from factory. Better, pricier machines typically have more accurately set OPVs, or these can be changed relatively easily. In some cases the work involved isn't difficult, but does involve opening up the machine, which may invalidate a warranty.

One final aspect of vibration pumps that is worth noting is the noise. The sound of them building pressure isn't particularly quiet or pleasant, though once they've built the pressure they are generally less noisy. If you (or others in your household) prize a sense of quiet and calm in the early morning, then it might be worth considering other options.

4. Rotary Pumps

Rotary pumps are the standard for most commercial machines. They're quieter and are also designed to be run for longer during the day. The downside of them is that they require motors to turn the pump head and these motors tend to be fairly large. Even some commercial manufacturers choose to leave the rotary pump outside of the machine, designing them to be stored in the cupboard underneath the machine.

There are some with smaller motors designed to fit inside smaller, semi-commercial espresso machines and adjusting the pump pressure on them is relatively easy to do. They do add a significant cost to a machine, and they don't necessarily produce 'better' pressure than any other system. They're highly repeatable, which is why they're preferred in commercial environments, but know that any machine that has one will take up more space in your kitchen or coffee-making area.

PRESSURE PROFILING

I should note here how machines achieve pressure profiling. There are several different approaches and using technologies like vibration pumps is not uncommon. Commercially you do also see the usage of gear pumps to create varying pressure, a component that is controlled by varying the voltage sent to it to vary how fast it turns and how much it produces. In other cases the pressure is controlled by effectively varying the over pressure valve, causing a varying amount of pressure to leak out of the system.

Machines that offer pressure profiling are often more expensive, and also frequently more complex to use and to dial in. There are benefits to being able to manipulate and vary the pressure during the shot, which are discussed in more detail in Brew Temperatures and Pump Pressures, pages 161–3.

How a Machine Heats Water

A lot of focus on espresso-brewing technology from the 2000s onward has been on brew temperature.

In particular, there was a strong desire to create a flatline temperature profile for espresso brewing, where the water passing through the coffee maintained a very narrow band of temperature. This pushed espresso-machine manufacturers to improve the technologies they used, and now many machines are capable of brewing at very consistent temperatures.

Personally, my priority for great espresso is not an absolutely flat temperature profile, but a repeatable one. Temperature undeniably impacts flavour, and so having the temperature be inconsistent will prevent you from reproducing the qualities of an espresso that you particularly love. However, if the machine produces a temperature profile, perhaps starting hot and cooling slightly toward the end of the shot, then this is no bad thing on the condition that it does this every single time.

With a domestic machine you are somewhat restricted by the physics involved, and the power supply you have available. Many machines may heat water efficiently but the mass of water they can heat from cold to the desired temperature is constrained by the element they use for heating, which in turn is constrained by the wattage available to them from your kitchen socket.

How a machine heats water tends to have a strong correlation to price, and is often the primary technology you are buying. The way it heats water will also impact the way you can control the machine's brewing temperature as well as the profile of temperature it produces.

Thermoblocks

Common in many cheaper machines is thermoblock technology. Here the element heats a mass of metal, and the water passes through a winding pathway inside it and is heated along its journey to the desired temperature. This is a cost-effective solution that is not inherently flawed but is limited in some ways.

How a manufacturer chooses to monitor and control the temperature of the thermoblock has an impact, and the speed at which the water passes through the system will impact its end temperature. Pushing a lot of cold water through the system rapidly, when you flush the group head with the portafilter out, will cool the system down very quickly. Leaving water inside the thermoblock for long periods may result in the water getting too

Sage Dual Boiler

Gaggia Classic

Victoria Arduino Prima

hot, and so often there's a balancing act. This means that you may want to flush out some water to cool down the machine, but ideally not too much. This balancing act is referred to as 'temperature surfing'.

Typically the same thermoblock is used to generate steam too, and in these situations there is a switch on the machine to set the thermostat to a much higher temperature. This means you can either use the machine for making espresso or for steaming milk, but not both at the same time.

In cheaper machines this is not a well-tuned technology, and your brewing temperature is more work to try to control and make repeatable. It is possible to get good results, but it will require more effort.

Single Boilers

These work, in many ways, similarly to thermoblock machines but instead of having the water pass through a block of metal, you have a larger volume of water held at a specific temperature.

Like thermoblock machines, these can only offer brewing water or steam at any particular time, but not both. The upside of these is that they tend to be a little more repeatable, and don't suffer quite as much variance as cheaper thermoblock set-ups.

Heat Exchangers

Probably the most common technology in higher-end domestic machines, and also in commercial machines, heat exchangers are built around a single boiler. That boiler runs at a high temperature, meaning that steam is always available. The water for coffee brewing passes through the steam boiler inside separate piping. As it passes through the heat from the steam, the heat surrounding the pipe is conducted to the brewing water and that brings it up to brewing temperature. Like a thermoblock, the speed at which the water passes through the system determines how hot it gets. This means that many heat-exchanger machines have a secondary system called a thermosyphon. This allows water to recirculate from the top of the heat exchanger to the group head and then back into the system just before the heat exchange happens.

As hotter water is lower in density it rises inside the system, creating a flow inside it, which causes water to constantly circulate. This movement of water also helps maintain the temperature of the group head, which would otherwise become cold and negatively impact the coffee brewing.

The most popular set-up like this was pioneered and popularized in a machine built by a company called FAEMA: the E61. It was named after the solar eclipse of its year of release: 1961. The E61-style group head is still popular in machines today, though there are other heat-exchanger systems and technologies in use.

Typically heat exchangers don't produce flatline temperature profiles, though some have been modified to do so. They can still benefit from a temperature-surfing routine to get the very best out of them too. Finally, when it comes to controlling them, you'll see a couple of approaches. The cheaper option is a simple mechanical thermostat that is difficult to set accurately and requires adjustment with a screwdriver. The second, and increasingly popular, option is digital control. These are often described as being PID controls, which relates to the maths used by a processor to accurately control the temperature. Ultimately it could easily be called digital temperature control. Here you're often adjusting the temperature of the steam boiler, so some level of conversion is required. A steam boiler may need to be set to 120°C (248°F) in order to produce brew water of 93°C (199°F), and in many cases a manufacturer will offer guidance on the corresponding steam temperature for your desired brew temperature. In other cases no guidance is given, and I'd recommend searching out discussion of the machine on consumer coffee forums online.

Dual Boilers

The rise of dual-boiler machines in cafés corresponded not with better espresso, but with larger milk drinks. As espresso began to be exported around the world under the Americanized quick-service restaurant model, and cappuccinos were offered in increasingly voluminous cups, cafés needed a lot more steam to produce the drinks. Heat exchangers had been built with traditional Italian espresso in mind, the barista steaming smaller quantities of milk and serving more straight espresso. When you increased the temperature of the steam boiler, to help the machine keep up with demand, then you increased your brewing temperature and that made your coffee taste worse.

Dual-boiler machines were the solution to that particular problem, but for the passionate espresso consumer they also opened up new possibilities. These machines have a dedicated steam boiler and then one or more boilers entirely separately, which are held at the desired brewing temperature. Separating the two requirements gave a lot of control to espresso-brewing temperatures and technologies quickly adopted a PID-style digital control of the brew boiler to increase accuracy.

These are, typically, more expensive machines for the café or home because you've got more boilers, more elements and more electronics inside. These machines also typically produce more flatline-style brew temperatures as you're drawing from a reservoir of water held at a specific temperature.

Brewing Controls

For some, espresso brewing should be about absolute control, and it should be a very manual experience.

Others want the espresso machine to offer some assistance when it comes to maintaining consistency in brewing. Some machines can control the amount of liquid you get when you push a button and they do it in various ways.

Manual Control

The cheapest option is that the machine doesn't control the brewing water volume at all. There will be an off/on switch for the pump and it is up to you to determine when to stop your shot. Cheaper machines will offer no guidance at all, while some will have a shot clock to at least offer some idea of how long you've been brewing for.

Time-based Control

This is a relatively rare control method, and perhaps for good reason. The machine can be programmed to run for 30 seconds and then stop. Due to the nature of espresso brewing, variations in your dose, grind or puck preparation will mean you get big variances in the amount of liquid the machine can push through the coffee in that time frame. You can obviously keep it as a constant and adjust your dose and grind until you get your desired amount of liquid but some people don't find this particularly intuitive. The upside is that this is a simple process for a machine to control without the need for additional components, so it is a little cheaper.

Volume-based Control

This is probably the most common method of control in commercial machines, but the additional cost makes it relatively rare in domestic machines. The technology uses a flow meter in the system, which is like a little water wheel with a magnet on one of the spokes. As the wheel is spun by water passing by, the rotations of the wheel are counted by the magnet passing a detector. After a fixed number of revolutions, the machine will stop brewing, presuming a fixed volume of water has passed through the system.

These meters work pretty well, though very accurate versions are incredibly expensive, and so the ones used in coffee machines can have some variation. In addition, they are measuring how much water was sent to the coffee, and not how much passed through the puck and ended up in the cup.

When it comes to programming them, typically the machine will ask you to start and stop it and it will record what you did, then reproduce that. Some machines will display a conversion to millilitres and others

MANUAL

will display the number of rotations of the flow meter, which is both utterly abstract and thankfully rare.

Weight-based Control

This technology is the most precise, and repeatable, because it measures how much liquid is actually in the cup and uses that information to control and stop the shot. However, this is a more expensive approach and does require that you be mindful of the fact that your cups are sitting on a weighing scale. If you move the cup during brewing, the machine can't tell the difference between you pressing down slightly on the cups and espresso going into them. Once your brew is underway it is better not to interfere with the cups if at all possible.

Currently this is the newest technology and also probably the most expensive. Some machines can interact with smart scales via bluetooth, though this is also still relatively rare. It is definitely the most desirable from a control point of view, but may mot make financial sense for everyone.

Everything Else

Milk steaming: How a machine heats water will also be connected to the way it heats water for steaming milk. A thermoblock or single-boiler machine (as discussed on pages 173–76) needs to be put into steam mode to get hot enough to produce any steam, meaning that you can't both make coffee and steam milk. Often these machines produce less pressure of steam, making steaming a little more difficult.

Most espresso machines have a pretty standard steam wand, with a metal tip on the end with 1–4 holes in it. However, some manufacturers have created their own solutions to steam the milk for you. Most of these are plastic attachments that help incorporate air into the milk without the user having to do or think too much about it. These vary in quality, from terrible to OK. Most are annoying to clean and maintain. I wouldn't really recommend any of them highly, but if you do have one then generally I find following the manufacturer's instructions to the letter to be the best way to go.

I should point out that recently a few manufacturers have created automatic steam wands that look like standard steam wands, and to be honest the results have been very impressive. If you're not interested in learning how to steam milk, then I would recommend them as an alternative.

If a machine has a standard steam wand, then it should be possible to get great milk foam texture from it, but there will be some variance in how quickly it steams milk and how easy it is to get great texture. (For more on steaming milk, turn to page 190.)

Portafilter size: While this might seem like an esoteric point to consider, it has an impact on the upgradeability of the machine – and therefore how long you are likely to own it before trying to sell it so you can buy something fancier.

The most common size for espresso baskets is 58mm. This means that there are more accessories for this size than any other; there are more tampers to choose from, more precision baskets to try. Other common sizes include 57mm, 54mm, 53mm and 51mm. There are excellent machines that do not use 58mm baskets, so I don't want to discourage anyone from buying something with a different basket size – but it is important to understand the impact of the decision.

Smart features/bluetooth connectivity: In the kitchen, smart devices are more often than not a waste of time and money, and in most cases I'd recommend some hesitancy around any internet-connected devices. That isn't to say that there are no connected devices that are well made, robust and secure, but they are few and far between.

The one useful feature worth checking for is a built-in clock and function to automatically turn on the machine. Most espresso machines need 20 minutes or more to get fully hot. Not having one isn't a deal-breaker though – a simple timer plug is usually enough to fix the problem.

How to Make Espresso

Now I'm going to discuss the actual process of making espresso. This is a combination of straight instructions, with a wider discussion about why you're doing what you're doing.

At first, this section might seem like an unnecessary complication of the espresso process, but I'm actually aiming for the opposite of that. I want to take away the superstitious ritualism that clings to espresso and aim to explain things that have the biggest return on cup quality.

My goal is to do the least possible in the espresso-brewing process, while still getting the best quality I can.

I've broken this down into four key stages that cover the linear chronological process of making great espresso: dosing and grinding; distribution; tamping; and, finally, extraction.

I'd make sure you have read the previous sections in this chapter, particularly The Principles of Espresso, pages 148–53, and also How to Adjust a Grinder, pages 158–59, before you begin this one.

1. DOSING AND GRINDING

Start the process by deciding a dose of ground coffee. For a double basket, that might range from 14g to 22g. Precision manufactured baskets will have a suggested dose, and I wouldn't vary from it by more than a gram. If you dose above this you won't be able to grind fine enough to have a good extraction, and if you dose below this the brew will be fine but the puck will be pretty messy afterwards, which is just inconvenient and annoying.

How you control your dose will depend on your grinder. Generally, I would recommend a single-dose grinder intended to grind the entirety of the bean dose you give it. There are grind-to-order grinders with hoppers designed to be full, and they will dose either by time or by weight.

With a single-dose grinder you should weigh your coffee right before grinding, and if your grinder suffers from static, then give it a spray with a misting bottle full of water. This reduces static dramatically when grinding.

You can double check the dose after grinding. If your grinder is consistent in how little coffee it retains, then you don't have to worry about this step long term, though with many grinders it is worth doing each time. With a grind-to-order grinder with a hopper, then I'd recommend weighing after grinding every single time.

1 Weigh your beans.

2 Spritz your beans with water before grinding to help avoid static.

3 It is a good idea to weigh your ground coffee.

2. DISTRIBUTION

This is perhaps the most important part of the brewing process (outside of getting the grind right for a particular dose). The evenness of the extraction is determined by distribution, which has a massive impact on how good your resulting espresso tastes.

Most grinders benefit from not grinding directly into the portafilter, even though many are designed to do exactly that. Grinding into a dosing cup, giving it a shake and then transferring to the portafilter is often beneficial in helping break up any clumps of ground coffee.

Alternatively, you can do this in the basket with a WDT (Weiss Distribution Technique) tool. You can buy these, 3D print them or just make one out of a wine cork and some needles used for cleaning 3D printers. You can use these to not only break up any clumps but also work the ground coffee until it is evenly distributed across the basket.

There are distribution tools that have little fins which you sit on the basket and rotate. I remain unconvinced by these as they tend to impact the top third of the puck, rather than the whole thing. I've had better results from WDT tools pretty consistently. If you use and find a benefit from a rotary distribution tool, then I wouldn't necessarily advise you to stop using it, but given the choice of tools I'd go for the more effective (and often cheaper) option.

1 Ground coffee may not be evenly distributed in the portafilter basket.

2 A WDT tool can help break up any clumps of coffee.

3 Your ground coffee should be evenly distributed within the portafilter basket before brewing.

3. TAMPING

Historically, tamping was an aspect of espresso making that was over-emphasized. The goal is to press out as much air as possible from the puck of coffee, and make sure that the bed of grounds is even and level. When you look at it from this angle, then tamping becomes more binary than granular. You have done it well or you have not; you have pressed hard enough to feel that the puck is fully compressed or you have not. How hard is hard enough? You'll see various metrics offered, such as 15kg of force. As an actual target, that isn't a bad one, but it is hard to know what that is or what it feels like without lugging a bathroom scale on to your kitchen worktop – and I'm not sure I endorse the effort for the limited reward. My slightly simplistic metric is to push until the coffee no longer feels soft and squishy. It seems absurd in a way, but it also works pretty well.

For many people new to espresso it can be tempting to blame tamping for the variance in their pours, but it is more likely coming from somewhere else. That doesn't mean that tamping is never the cause or the source of coffee brewing problems. The first thing to make sure of is that you get a tamper that properly fits the basket you are using. The more precise the fit, the better, and most precision basket manufacturers will offer exact size recommendations for tamper bases for their baskets.

1 Make sure your tamper fits the portafilter as precisely as possible and press down until the coffee no longer feels soft and squishy.

2 Feel the top of the tamper base with your fingertips to check it is flat and even.

Aside from the base size, you should make sure you have a tamper that fits your hand well. A tamper should be gripped a little like a door handle, and when you tamp, your elbow should be directly above your wrist. This will allow you to safely apply force without causing potential wrist injuries – a very real concern, especially for professional baristas. You may benefit from imagining a screw sticking out of a worktop, and mimicking how you would hold a screw driver to best give it one last turn (without doing any actual twisting!).

Once you've pressed the tamper in completely, you can use your fingertips to feel the top of the tamper base against the walls of the basket to check that the tamper is nice and flat and even. Small adjustments can happen now – getting the bed level is very important for water flowing through it all evenly. You'll see some people twist or spin the tamper at this point. I picked up this habit early in my career and it has proven hard to shake, even though it makes no difference and adds no benefit. If you can avoid adding one more step to your routine, then I'd recommend that. The goal should always be the simplest, easiest route to espresso.

Make sure no loose grounds are sitting on the rim of the basket and then you're ready to head to the next step.

4. EXTRACTION

Before you load the portafilter, with many machines there can be a benefit to a quick flush of water from the group head. This is done in commercial environments to rinse off any grounds that have remained on the dispersion screen from the previous shot, but you may have a clean screen to start with. In this case, the flush often helps stabilize the temperature of the machine. Some machines may run hot, and the flush will cool them slightly, and some work the opposite way. This process of temperature surfing is thankfully being slowly eradicated by better heating technologies. It is a frustrating and wasteful practice, wasting both water and energy, and knowing the exact amount to flush out to get the temperature you want also takes time, experimentation and sometimes some temperature-measuring equipment.

Best practice says not to leave the coffee in the group head long without brewing. The longer the coffee sits there the hotter it becomes, and this means that the overall temperature of brewing gets a touch hotter and the coffee can start to taste bitter as a result. Realistically you've got 20–30 seconds before you should worry too much, but being consistent in your routine is the important thing, so generally I'd still advise brewing as soon as you've locked in your handle.

Your scales should be nearby and with most machines you have 5–10 seconds from pushing the brew button until coffee appears. This is enough time to put the scales on the drip tray, put the cup on top and to zero the scales.

However, coffee making should be fun and not a test, so if you would prefer to get everything ready before hitting brew, then that is no bad thing.

If your machine has a built-in brew timer that's great; if not, then many coffee scales have timers or you could use your phone. Recording brew time is useful. Start recording the time from the minute you turn on the brewing switch. This is the true brew time: the moment coffee and water begin their contact. You'll see some people advise timing from liquid appearing, but I would strongly recommend timing from pushing brew. General advice says traditional espresso will take 25–35 seconds to brew. There are many, many examples of excellent espresso recipes that are both quicker and slower. However, I'd recommend getting very comfortable with the base line espresso recipe before experimenting too much with more advanced approaches.

Some machines will stop themselves based on either time, volume of water pumped or, very rarely, by weight of liquid in the cup (as discussed on pages 178–80). Most machines require stopping manually. With most scales I'd recommend stopping around 2g away from your target liquid weight for your chosen recipe. Remember, there is still liquid espresso on the way to the cup, and some scales will have a bit of lag as well. After a handful of espressos you'll know exactly where to stop your set of scales in order to get the weight you need.

If you have a naked portafilter, then you can watch the extraction, and you'll be able to see any obvious channels. In some cases you'll see sections of a dramatically lighter colour, and worst-case scenario you'll see a tiny jet of liquid coffee spray off at an angle, indicating quite a bad channel. With a spouted portafilter it is harder to see, unless things go very wrong and the brewing espresso looks extremely watery when it shouldn't.

In theory, a naked portafilter is therefore superior, but it does have a couple of drawbacks. Firstly, you can't split the shots and produce two single espressos – sometimes it is nice to share! Secondly, in every extraction

you'll see some flaws and, depending on your personality and approach to espresso, this may rob you of some of the pleasure of the espresso. It is useful diagnostically, no question, but sometimes it is OK just to look at it, think it looks beautiful and not worry too much more about it.

When brewing is finished, you're welcome to enjoy the espresso straight away, but it is worth getting the used coffee puck out of the machine relatively quickly. Once it is knocked out, I'd also give the screen a flush. (I'll discuss a wider cleaning and maintenance routine on pages 214–18.)

Steaming Milk

In this section I'll discuss the theory of milk steaming before diving into the technique.

A drink made with properly steamed milk is a wonderful thing, adding sweetness and incredible texture to the coffee. Great milk foam is called microfoam, because you're producing bubbles that are so small they're barely visible. The smaller any bubble is, the stronger it is, and microfoamed milk will produce a drink that has great texture from start to finish: marshmallowy soft, creamy, light but rich. Understanding the goal helps to grasp the technique, and then once you understand the science you can produce the exact texture you want with ease and diagnose issues with texture or steaming more easily.

Why Milk Foams

I'm going to cover a little science of foam here, which applies to various kinds of dairy and non-dairy milks. For something to foam you need two things: some way of adding air bubbles to the liquid, and something inside the liquid that will act as a foaming agent, trapping the air in stable bubbles. In most milks this is a protein of some sort.

Proteins are built of building blocks called amino acids. Some of these building blocks have parts that are repelled by water (hydrophobic) and under most circumstances these blocks end up facing each other, which

is part of the reason that proteins often have twisting, convoluted shapes. When you physically stress these proteins, by either heat or mechanical action (like whisking), then you denature them enough that the hydrophobic parts are separated. They are now looking for anything that isn't water, and an air bubble is perfect. This causes the protein to wrap itself around the air bubble with all the hydrophobic parts facing the air and the rest of the protein facing the water around the bubble. This kind of protein is called a surface active agent, often shortened to surfactant.

If you've ever cooked meringues and made the mistake of getting some yolk into your egg white mix, you'll know that fat can play a negative role in foam formation. The fat competes with the air for the attention of the hydrophobic parts of the protein, and this is why fat can inhibit foam formation or cause it to break down more quickly.

When it comes to steaming dairy milk for drinks, the fat content plays a dual role. Skimmed milk will take on air more easily and produce a more stable foam than whole milk. That doesn't mean making great drinks with skimmed milk is easier than whole milk, and for many people the opposite is true.

NON-DAIRY MILK ALTERNATIVES

For those looking for an alternative to dairy in their coffee, there have never been more alternatives. For a long time, soy milk was considered the de facto alternative choice in coffee shops, but oat milk has seen huge growth in the last few years. There are several different brands doing great work, but what I'd recommend is seeking out products designed specifically for coffee if you want to bring one into your home coffee routine. Many of the non-dairy alternatives are designed for more traditional uses – on cereal or in general cooking/baking – and these generally don't taste quite right or steam quite right with coffee. Most brands produce a coffee-focused version, and among those you'll find some aiming to be closer to dairy in taste and texture, and others trying to just be better at pairing with coffee. I'd encourage tasting a few to find one that fits your personal tastes.

Fat also changes the texture of the drink, as well as the flavour release of the coffee. Fat slows flavour release, and reduces its intensity. A skimmed-milk cappuccino will have a more intense coffee flavour, but it won't linger. A whole-milk version will have less intense peak of coffee-ness, but that flavour will last longer in the mouth.

The fat in dairy milk is often the cause of milk that doesn't foam well, no matter what you do. Most of the fat in dairy milk is in a configuration called a triglyceride. This means it is shaped like a weird letter E, with a backbone of glycerol and three fatty acids coming off it. When this triglyceride breaks down you'll have three free fatty acids, and some glycerol. Glycerol is highly competitive with air for the attention of the proteins and causes the foam you've created to fail quickly. Milk where the fat has broken down will almost fizz (you can hear it clearly if you hold the milk jug to your ear after steaming), and your small bubbles of microfoam seem to quickly form larger and larger bubbles. The milk may not necessarily taste bad, but no matter what you do it will never produce great microfoam. This is sometimes caused by the herd's diet, but more often it is a result of improper storage. As charming as it is, I'd avoid milk in clear glass bottles. Direct sunlight in particular can quickly cause issues with milk's foamability, without impacting its taste too much.

Temperature

One of the historical points of tension in a coffee shop has come from customers wanting hotter drinks and baristas not wanting to make the drink too hot. This really comes down to a flaw in milk. The proteins involved in milk foaming begin to permanently denature and break down as the milk begins to exceed 68°C (154°F). The hotter you go, the more the proteins break down, and in doing so they produce a worse texture but also begin to break apart and produce new flavours and aromas. The smell of cooked milk is quite distinctive and comes in part from the release of hydrogen sulfide as amino acids break apart. This is why it has that cooked eggy smell, or reminds some people of baby sick.

It is worth noting that the breakdown is a function of both temperature and time. If you heated milk up to 60°C (140°F), let it cool completely and then steamed it a second time, you'd start to perceive the smells and tastes of the proteins breaking down at lower temperatures. Long-life milk is pasteurized at much higher temperatures than this but the milk is held there for only 1–2 seconds before being chilled.

All this means that the best-tasting milk drinks have a ceiling to their temperature. For some people a hotter drink is more important than a delicious drink, but most people are happier with a slightly less hot drink that has a sweetness and delightful texture. A temperature of 60°C (140°F) is hotter than is comfortable for immediate drinking for many people, and often the mindset shift is about how long they should wait before diving in rather than trying to get the drink to be hotter in the first place.

In my experience, temperature impacts flavour and texture with dairy-alternative milks too. It isn't quite the same as with dairy; the cooked milk smell is obviously different, but it does seem like some of the proteins present are breaking down and releasing new aromas. The texture doesn't seem to hold up quite as well at higher temperatures either.

It is also important to emphasize how useful, if not completely essential, it is to start with the milk at refrigerator temperature (around 4°C/39°F). This really makes the whole process of steaming milk far easier and sets you up for better success.

The Milk-steaming Technique

The technique for steaming milk should result in a delicious milk drink, with natural sweetness and pleasing texture that comes from the foam being made of bubbles so small that they're almost impossible to see. Within this process you have three tasks: adding air to the milk, creating the best possible foam texture and, perhaps most importantly, heating the milk.

It is helpful to think of these as discrete tasks, because when you steam milk you tackle each of them in different ways and at different times in the process. Obviously when using a steam wand, you're going to be heating the milk the entire time, regardless of what else you're doing, but you can break the process down into two stages:

Phase One: Blowing Bubbles

This phase is often called 'stretching the milk', a term that seems to have stuck inside the English-speaking coffee industry. What you're aiming to do here is to use the force of the steam leaving the wand to drag and push air down into the milk. This will happen when the tip of the wand sits on the very surface of the milk. You can see and hear this happening: the milk will begin to expand inside the jug (hence the idea of stretching the milk) and you'll hear a slurping sound too.

When you start steaming milk, one of the decisions you should have made beforehand is about the amount of foam you're trying to make. If you want a traditional cappuccino with a thick, moussey layer of foam, then you'll need to add more air in this phase than if you want to make a flat white, which has a much thinner layer of microfoam.

It is difficult to give you precise instructions when it comes to telling you how much air to add to the milk in this first stage. I would say a 10–20 per cent increase in volume will give you suitable milk for a latte or flat white, and will also allow you to pour latte art should you wish to learn that skill. If you're making a more traditional cappuccino, then an increase of something like 50–60 per cent is a good place to start. This will be thick, marshmallowy foam, and it will be wonderful. There is no absolute standard for milk drinks, and part of the pleasure of a home espresso set-up is developing the skills to produce the drink you most enjoy, so the time spent in trial and error is completely worthwhile.

It is vital that this phase is completed before the milk is really warm to the touch. The

---

KNOW YOUR WAND

The technique I'm giving on these pages is for use with a traditional steam wand. It is usually a stainless-steel wand with a tip screwed on to the end that has between one and four little holes in it. The steam may be controlled via a knob or a button. If you have a steam wand that is notably different to this, then it may be a proprietary technology and the best thing you can do is to follow the steps in the user manual as closely as you can. However, understanding the technique the device is trying to replicate is helpful in potentially diagnosing issues you may have.

quicker this can happen, the better it will be, because you'll have longer for the next phase, which is all about texture.

Phase Two: The Hot Whisk

The second phase of milk steaming is all about taking the bubbles you made in the first phase and smashing them down to as small a size as possible. To do this the tip of the wand needs to be just under the surface, submerged just past the point at which it joins on to the main wand. Do not put it to the bottom of the jug.

With the wand below the surface, steam can churn and roll the milk around in the jug. This phase should be very quiet; you don't want to hear any slurps or even sips of air. You want to see a vortex forming in the centre of the jug, and you'll see it drag larger bubbles into it as steaming progresses. The longer you can spend doing this, the better the end texture will be. As you have a fixed end point of temperature, this means moving into the second phase as quickly as possible.

The position of the wand in the jug is key. If it isn't in the right place, then it will be difficult to get the milk to spin around and form the vortex necessary. I'll cover a step by step overleaf, but during this phase you should be watching to make sure a vortex is forming, and adjusting the position of the wand in your jug until you see things acting as they should.

To show this process in action I have used water instead of milk, as milk would not allow visibility of the wand or the bubbles.

STEP BY STEP

1 Find an appropriately sized stainless-steel milk pitcher. Your desired portion of milk should not fill it above the bottom of the pouring spout.

Make sure the milk you're using is refrigerator cold. If you want to minimize waste, then there's nothing wrong with weighing your desired amount.

Make sure the machine is at a suitable temperature to produce steam. Some machines require additional heating for this phase.

Just before steaming, point the steam wand over the drip tray and open the valve. This will purge out any condensation, and you should see a relatively dry steam. Holding your cleaning cloth around the wand will help minimize the mess. Be careful: steam is hot.

Pull the steam wand toward you, so that it is at around a 45-degree angle away from the machine.

Before you start steaming: Make your espresso first. It can sit while you steam the milk. It won't go off or notably decline in quality. It will cool down a bit, but it is going to be diluted by a good amount of hot milk that should balance out the temperature drop nicely.

2 With the spout of the jug pointing forward (use the spout as a guide for the steam wand), bring the jug up until the tip of the wand is submerged in the milk, but go no deeper.

Tilt the jug slightly to the side, keeping the wand in the spout of the jug.

Open the steam wand fully.

Immediately lower the jug to bring the wand's tip to the very top of the milk – you want it almost as if it is sitting on top of the milk. You should hear a slurping sound as you add the desired amount of air.

As soon as the required amount of air has been added, raise the jug up slightly to submerge the wand in the milk by a few centimetres.

Do not put the wand to the bottom of the jug.

3 Make sure that a vortex has formed in the milk; you may need to tilt the jug further to the side. You should see the milk spinning around aggressively.

When you reach your desired temperature, stop steaming. Many people use their hand on the side of the jug to gauge the temperature. Most people have a heat tolerance of around 55°C (131°F), and so steaming for 3–5 seconds past the point of the jug being uncomfortable to hold is a good guideline for most machines. Some trial and error to find your preferred temperature is necessary.

As soon as you've stopped steaming, put the pitcher to the side and focus on cleaning the wand. Use a damp cloth to wipe any milk from the wand, then point it over the drip tray again and open the steam valve briefly to purge any milk that might have been retained.

Thermometers: There are a variety of milk-steaming thermometers available, but most of the cheap dial ones are very slow and not particularly accurate. A digital thermometer works very well, but I understand that asking people to probe their steamed milk might be going too far. Even for me.

4 Your steamed milk is not quite ready to pour yet. Tap it gently on the counter or worktop a couple of times, as this will burst any remaining large bubbles (above left).

Only once the large bubbles have been burst should you swirl the milk in the jug. You want to whip the liquid milk up into the foam above, but you don't want to make any new bubbles in the process. The swirling is reminiscent of our most practised and serious wine-glass swirl. You'll know the milk is ready to pour when it looks like gloss paint (above right).

Pour into your coffee and enjoy.

MILK – A FEW SUGGESTIONS
FOR PROBLEM-SOLVING

The biggest challenge most people have is getting the texture they want, often ending up with bigger bubbles in their microfoam than they'd like. Here are a few possible causes:

Air was added too late in the process, so there wasn't enough time in the second phase (see page 199) to whisk it down to tiny bubbles. Try to be a bit more aggressive earlier on when adding air to the milk.

Sufficient steam pressure was not used. If you've only partly opened the valve, then it is very difficult to get good milk texture. If the machine is underpowered on heating the steam boiler to a high enough temperature, then this may also be the issue. If you find your steam wand too aggressive, especially for smaller milk drinks, then I'd recommend changing the tip to one that lets out a lower volume of steam but keeps the same pressure. These are often called 'low flow' tips. They may have less holes or smaller holes than the factory standard. If you're often steaming less than 100ml of milk, then I'd strongly recommend getting one for your machine. The threading on the tips is often fairly standard, so replacement parts aren't difficult to find.

Alternatively, milk that isn't in great condition will have foam that looks good initially but very quickly starts to collapse into bigger bubbles. If you hold it to your ear you can actually hear it fizz like a soft drink. This milk probably tastes fine, and if it is in date, then I'd say it is safe to consume for other uses. However, some of its fats have probably broken down and this is causing the foam to fail.

Take One Espresso...

Espresso Drinks and Recipes

In this section I want to cover a selection of espresso-based drinks and try to convey the idea behind them.

It isn't really possible to offer up a definitive recipe for a cappuccino, any more than one could offer up a definitive recipe for a lasagne, but with a little history and context I hope you can understand what the recipe is trying to achieve, to allow you to create your own ideal version of the drink – or drinks – you enjoy.

Espresso

Espresso is a small, strong cup of coffee brewed under high pressures. It is distinguished not only by its intensity but also by a layer of red-brown foam that sits on top called crema. The idea of espresso dates back to the turn of the twentieth century, with new machines able to rapidly brew strong cups of filter-style coffee using trapped steam pressure to press the water through the coffee quickly. The name comes from the fact that, much like in English, the Italian word for 'rapid' and 'pressed out' is the same. In English we would have an express train, and we would also use the word 'express' to mean 'press out'.

Modern espresso dates back to 1948, to the espresso machine that was named for Achille Gaggia that used a lever to compress a large spring, and this spring would then be used to push hot water through coffee using a piston mechanism. This was the first time espresso was brewed under very high pressures –

around 9 bars or even higher – and so was the first time the drink was topped with its distinctive foam. Gaggia's customers were sceptical of this new froth on their coffee, so he described it as '*crema caffe naturale*' – natural coffee cream. It was a stroke of marketing genius.

In the speciality coffee movement it becomes a little trickier to define the espresso recipe because the standard has become brewing a double espresso, rather than a single. Most espresso recipes you'll see from roasters or online presume you're using the double basket and will probably be combining both espressos in one cup to drink. For this reason the standard Italian espresso recipe, which is for a single espresso, seems very far away from what people talk about online.

Espresso con Panna

This is a simple but quite delicious recipe. A small amount of whipped cream is added to the espresso. Best enjoyed stirred in a little, but with enough cool cream floating on top to contrast with the rich, hot coffee below.

Macchiato

Macchiato translates from Italian into English as 'marked' or 'stained'. The drink was born in the busy espresso bar in Italy, where espressos were often brewed quickly and set up on the counter in a line to be collected by patrons. If someone asked for a little dash of milk to be added to theirs it created a small problem because the crema on top would disguise which was the one with milk. To solve this problem baristas started adding a small spoonful of milk foam to mark which was the drink with a little milk in it.

The more modern version is quite different, often an espresso cup filled to the brim with steamed milk. This comes more from baristas wanting to show off and to pour latte art in small cups than it does from creating the best drink possible. The ratio ends up being close to 1:1 coffee to milk. Both versions can be very enjoyable, but there is now some confusion around which to expect when you order.

There is further confusion in the coffee world due to the introduction of a drink in Starbucks called the Caramel Macchiato. This has been a huge success for the company, but has set another expectation for what a macchiato should be that is a long way from the first two. Starbucks's Caramel Macchiato is a large latte that is marked, or stained, with caramel sauce.

Espresso Romano

Not often seen, but worth experimenting with if you like the sound of it. Traditionally it is an espresso served with either a small lemon slice or a twist of lemon zest. If you're looking to recreate this drink, then choosing which one to add should probably be guided by the style of espresso you're drinking. A little lemon slice might add some nice acidity to a darker roast, but would make a lighter roast unpleasantly sour and unbalanced. As a zest twist is really all lemon aroma without any impact on acidity, then it is probably the safer choice and likely to add some lovely aromatic complexity to the drink.

Cortado

This is another drink where you'll see some pretty big variations, especially between the traditional versions and the more modern interpretations. In the past the drink was most commonly seen in Spain and Portugal. It was a 1:1 ratio of coffee and steamed milk, served in a larger glass. The style of espresso brewed in that region was a little longer and more diluted than was traditional in Italy, which was part of the drink's character.

In a modern speciality shop it is hard to predict what you'll get. It could be anything from a 1:1 ratio up to a 1:3 ratio of espresso to milk. Often this correlates to whether or not the barista is pouring latte art in the drink.

Piccolo Latte

Within coffee it isn't unusual to see Italian words used for drink names that aren't ever really seen or served in Italy, and this is a good example. It was most likely invented outside Italy, but given an Italian name to convey some sort of authenticity or set an expectation. The name suggests a small caffe latte and that's pretty much what you'll get. This is most often served in a glass, with a 1:3 to 1:4 ratio of coffee to milk. The milk is usually steamed to create just a thin layer of foam on the drink.

Americano

The story you'll hear is that after World War II, American soldiers stationed in Italy asked for their espresso to be watered down. However, espresso as we know it wasn't invented until 1948 and wasn't popularized for some years afterwards. The name of this coffee is more likely due to a watered-down espresso being closer in strength to filter coffee, which people associated with American coffee preferences.

The recipe is one or two shots of espresso, diluted by hot water. You can do hot water first and espresso on top, or the other way around without impacting the taste too much. I prefer hot water first because the drink just looks much nicer. And if you haven't tried skimming the crema off the top of an americano before drinking it, then you should – it reduces the bitterness quite nicely, making for a better drink. A typical ratio of coffee to water in an americano can go from 1:3 to 1:6, and really is about personal preference.

Long Black

This is a very similar coffee to an americano on paper, but comes from a different place. This drink is commonly seen in Australia and New Zealand. It was traditionally brewed with a double ristretto (see page 156), from a fairly large dose of coffee – this was the style of espresso popular at the time. As a result, the drink is often strong, rich and intense. Ratios of 1:3 to 1:4 are common.

The Cappuccino

It may seem quintessentially Italian, but the cappuccino originated in Austria. In the old Viennese coffee houses of the late 1800s there was a drink called a *kapuziner*. The waiter would mix coffee and milk until it was the same brown as a Capuchin monk's robes. A fairly esoteric colour choice, but it was also used outside coffee shops for a specific shade of brown. By specifying colour the customer was indicating a preference for the coffee's strength and flavour.

As espresso machines rose in popularity, so too did the practice of using some of the trapped steam in them to heat, and foam, milk. The idea at the root of the cappuccino stayed the same; this was about a coffee and milk drink that had a strong coffee flavour.

At some point there came a rule of thirds, that cappuccino should be 1 part espresso, 1 part milk, 1 part foam. This feels neat and

easy, but would make a traditional single shot cappuccino about a 75ml drink. Which it is not, and has never been. I suspect the idea someone was trying to communicate was that the espresso should be mixed with milk foamed in such a way that when you poured it you had equal parts foam and milk. (Thus it is confusing, but correct, to say that cappuccino is an espresso mixed with equal parts foam and milk.) In most of Italy, a single shot cappuccino is served in a 150ml cup and has a thick layer of delightful moussey foam, which makes sure the coffee flavour isn't too diluted. The most common recipe is a ratio of 1:3 to 1:4 coffee to milk, ideally with at least 1–2cm of foam on top.

The modern speciality coffee shop has really blurred the lines on what a cappuccino is, with many serving small, very strong milk drinks with varying amounts of foam. And then there are very large and frothy monstrosities available at the larger chains.

Caffe Latte

While it may feel pretentious to order a caffe latte instead of just a latte, I have heard enough stories of people travelling to Italy and being served a glass of milk in response to make sure I call it by its proper name. What probably adds to the confusion of many an Italian barista is that the drink is not particularly common in Italy, and its origins are probably outside the country, with the name becoming Italianized later.

The idea of the caffe latte is simple – a sweet, milky beverage with a little coffee flavour. That is no bad thing. However, the stigma of it being a drink for people who aren't all that into coffee sadly remains. Regardless of stigma, it is probably the most popular coffee drink worldwide.

The rise of super automatic machines has buoyed the popularity of the latte macchiato, where the milk goes in first and the espresso

is gently layered in afterwards. This is sometimes seen in Italy, though often made with Moka-pot coffee in the home.

Most lattes have a double shot of espresso but are served in a larger cup to allow more milk, with it being typical to have a little milk foam, but not too much. Ratios can range from 1:4 to 1:7.

Flat White

The flat white's origins remain a source of contention between Australia and New Zealand, but I think it is safe to say that it is an Antipodean original. During the rise of speciality coffee, in many places the flat white became a quiet symbol of that modern movement, it's presence on a menu board being a surprisingly good indicator of quality. It didn't take long for it to be coopted by chains and those less interested in excellence.

Considering how it likely came about, this is an entertaining second lease of life for the drink. The original flat white was probably a response to the rise of the sea-foam cappuccino, heaped with questionable froth. People didn't want an airy cup of coffee and milk, they wanted a flat, white coffee. Thus the flat white was born, and it slowly evolved into a drink that is best described as a small, strong latte.

Usually no bigger than 150–180ml and always with a double espresso and milk steamed to have a thin layer of foam, the flat white has the textural qualities of a latte, with the coffee kick of a cappuccino. Ratios can go from the intense 1:2 up to 1:4 at a push, with 1:3 probably being the most common.

Caffe Corretto

For once, a drink in this list seen more commonly in Italy than outside of it. All the more delightful is the name for an espresso served with a little alcohol in it or on the side: corrected coffee. Often you'll see it served as an espresso with a little brandy, grappa or other spirit on the side. The coffee is drunk, often after dinner and often with a little sugar, and the booze is poured into the nearly empty cup, swirled around and then drunk. It is a fun ritual, and from a taste perspective can be more than the sum of its parts. It is also common to see it served with the booze already added to the coffee, for more of a little hot digestivo cocktail experience.

Mocha

We don't really know how this drink got its name. It's mostly described as a hot chocolate with a shot, or two, of espresso in it. Despite the fact that chocolate can be as complex and fascinating as coffee, full of terroir as well as flavours from the craftsmanship of the maker, it is another drink that is culturally maligned and unfairly dismissed as 'not serious' (as if seriousness were a useful indicator of delight or quality...). Most likely it got its name from the port of Mokka in Yemen. An early and popular combination of coffees in coffee's history is the Moka Java blend. Initially this contained coffees from these two origins, but soon became a stylistic shorthand for an earthy, chocolatey blend of other origins. Somehow this morphed into the drink we know today.

There are no real ratios agreed for a mocha; some are very chocolate heavy, some more coffee forward, sweetened and fattened up by the richness of the chocolate in the drink. Most, these days, have latte art on top, but beyond that it seems a much looser idea that you can experiment with to find what you most enjoy.

And more...

There are, of course, a variety of other drinks and recipes that are popular. I could have added a section on the Bicern, the Magic, the Gibraltar, the Red Eye and many more. There are some delightful localized espresso drinks, and finding and trying them is one of the delights of travel. Baristas who serve unusual drinks are usually very happy to talk about what they are and how they're made, should you wish to recreate them, but I don't think I can offer an exhaustive list here without turning this book into a research project that most people won't want to read!

Cleaning and Maintaining Your Equipment

When it comes to cleaning equipment, there is a bit of tension between the idea that there is no such thing as too clean for a coffee machine, and the problem of diminishing returns.

You could clean thoroughly every single day and your machinery and your taste buds would thank you for it, but I'm not sure that is the best use of your time.

There can be rules and recommendations for cafés, because those machines are used all day every day and need solid routines during the day, as well as at the end of the day, in order to prevent the rapid build-up of unpleasant flavours. The same is not true of the home machine. Here I'll discuss why machines need to be cleaned, how to do it, and then how to decide on the best cleaning routine for your own set-up.

Espresso Machines

There are a couple of reasons why espresso machines will need the most cleaning of any coffee equipment you'll have. Firstly, the nature of how most of them discharge pressure from the group head means that there is coffee residue inside the machine. When you're brewing under 9 bars, you've built up a lot of pressure against the coffee. In order to make the handle safe to remove after you finish brewing, most espresso machines have a valve in the group head that allows the

remaining pressure to exit up through the group head and then through a waste tube into the drip tray. This release of pressure is why a basket with a lower dose of coffee is a soupy, broken mess at the end of the shot. That release of pressure up into the group head essentially causes the cake to explode, and the more room it has to expand into, the bigger the mess it will make.

This upward release of pressure drags not only liquid coffee residue up into the group head but also some fine particles of ground coffee. This residue quickly dehydrates in the very hot group head, and will begin to accumulate. Rinsing immediately afterwards by flushing the group head does help but there will still be some build-up. It's easy to forget to do it straight away too, and many espresso machines are left on for quite a while after a shot is pulled (for example while you steam milk). The more coffee you make, the more residue you'll have, and the longer it spends cooking away inside the group head, the harder it is to remove with water alone and the more negative tastes it will add to your future espressos.

To clean a group head properly, you first need to drop down the shower screen, if this is done easily on your machine. Often there's a central screw holding the piece in place, and a mesh screen will drop down, and sometimes an additional metal block whose function is to help distribute the brew water over the puck during brewing (usually called a dispersion block). These should be taken to the sink (carefully, as they're hot) and scrubbed clean with soap. Dish-washing soap is fine, though ideally nothing too perfumed! You can also clean off any residue from the underside of the group head that the block sits against. Make sure no grounds are sitting on the rubber gasket in the group head too. Replace all the parts and then you can do a clean with espresso-machine cleaner that is called a backflush. You'll need a small amount of specific cleaner for espresso machines,

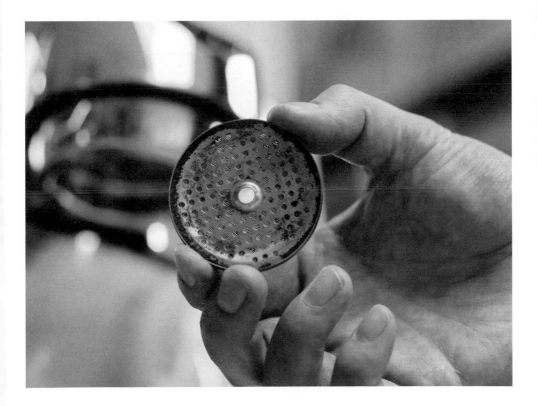

and a blank basket for the portafilter that has no holes in it. (If your machine didn't come with a blank basket, then stop reading and immediately go online and buy one.)

The important thing to remember about backflushing a machine is that the cleaning happens mostly when the group head isn't running. Initially when you lock it in and run the pump you'll start dissolving the powder, but there'll be little flow of the cleaner out of the basket. Once you stop the pump, the dissolved cleaning solution is pushed up into the group head where it can start to work on the residue. Generally a cycle of 5 seconds on, 10 seconds off repeated 5 or 6 times is a good place to start (unless the machine is in a terrible state). After this you can take the handle out, empty it and rinse it and then lock it back in to do a clean water flush and repeat the process of 5 seconds on, then 5 seconds off 5 or so times.

If you run the group head and you see any discolouration or smell any chemical, keep rinsing.

The real question is: how often should you do this routine? As I said at the start, an argument could be made for every single day, but if you brew just a couple of espressos each day, then this is probably overkill. I'd recommend daily flushing with water and then, depending on usage, you can do a chemical clean every 2, 3, 5 or 7 days. I can't give you the right frequency for your particular set-up. The acid test is pretty much: are you disgusted by the state of the block and screen when you drop them down? If so, then clean more frequently.

Grinders

Frequency of cleaning a grinder does, in part, come down to the make and model you're using. Some accumulate very fine particles

quite quickly, and this can cause the grinder to get hotter than desired (coffee powder is an excellent insulator) and can add unpleasant tastes to your brews. Additionally, some grinders are built to be opened frequently with limited risk of you damaging or misaligning parts which would impair the function and quality of the grinder.

You'll see some recommendations for using uncooked rice as a way of cleaning grinder burrs and burr chambers. I've never ever seen a grinder manufacturer recommend this method, and if you are going to try this, then know you're invalidating your warranty and do so at your own risk. I have seen a product that is basically coffee-bean shapes made out of a cleaning product. These work quite well, but are perhaps too expensive for regular use.

If you're comfortable doing so, then the best thing to do is to open the burr chamber and

vacuum out any remaining grounds and then get in there with a little brush to remove anything more stuck on. Pay particular attention to the exit chute where the coffee leaves the burr chamber. If your grinder has threading in the burr chamber, then be very careful not to get ground coffee into the threads. It makes for a miserable experience. If you're not comfortable opening your grinder fully, then giving it a proper vacuum now and again probably helps a little, and brush out whatever compressed and accumulated coffee grounds you can see.

External parts of a grinder should be cleaned regularly. If your grinder has a hopper, and you grind medium or darker roasts, then a layer of oil will build up on the hopper surprisingly quickly. Do not let it build up because it rapidly oxidizes and smells pretty terrible. If the hopper is easily removed, then give it a good wash with soapy water, rinse it thoroughly and dry it completely before putting it back together.

Brewers

Coffee-brewing machines are relatively easy to keep clean. The often overlooked places are the bottom of the brew basket and the carafe (if your machine has one). Because the materials used in most coffee brewers are dark coloured it can be easy to miss the accumulation of coffee residue in the filter basket and around the valve at the base of it, present in some machines. This will require a bit of scrubbing with a soapy scourer and a rinse, and is pretty easy work that's best done every week if you remember.

Carafes are often difficult to clean by hand. The best way to bring them back to delightfully clean is to put a heaped tablespoon (or coffee scoop if you want to give it some utility) of espresso-machine cleaner into the carafe and fill it with very hot water. It should dissolve completely as you add the water and you can just leave it for a few hours to soak (overnight is totally fine, nothing bad will happen) and then rinse it thoroughly. In most cases it will look brand new.

Descaling

Coffee-brewing water is not an easy topic, see the section on water on pages 41–8 for more information. Sadly, the best water for coffee brewing and water that produces limescale have some overlap, so for many, descaling is going to be part of coffee-equipment ownership. If you're descaling reasonably often, then the process is pretty painless. I recommend using citric acid as it is cheap, surprisingly easy to buy and food safe. I usually make a 5 per cent solution, though you could use a lower concentration if you're descaling often or your water is slow to form limescale.

Fill your machine with the descaling solution and turn it on. If it is a brewer, then you can run a brew cycle. If it is an espresso machine, then you can start to flush out the solution once the machine is hot. Once you've flushed through all the solution (1 litre is a good starting amount), then you'll want to run at least 1 litre of fresh, clean water through. Taste the water coming out at the end of this period, and if it has even a hint of lemony sharpness, then flush a little more through. (This is why using a food-safe descaler is useful).

If you've not descaled for a long time, then there is a risk in some machines of a larger piece of scale flaking off and clogging a narrow section of the hydraulic circuit of the machine. This will eventually dissolve but if you're having issues, then you might need a professional to isolate the section that has clogged and to remove it and clean it out manually before putting it all back together again. (Or, if you're comfortable, you can have a go, but please be cautious – opening up an espresso machine and taking it to pieces voids your warranty and messing around with any electrical appliance is incredibly dangerous if you don't know what you're doing.)

Even if your water is pretty soft, you may benefit from descaling once a year, and more frequently if your water is harder.

Index

Acknowledgements

I am hugely grateful to both Michael and Melinda for all the work they did to help make this book happen. Without their help, this would never have made it to print.

Thank you to everyone at my publisher, Octopus, for all their hard work in the shaping of the words and then their transformation of them into this beautiful book.

Thank you to the team at Square Mile Coffee Roasters for being a source of inspiration, challenging conversations and delicious coffee.

Thank you to my family.

Picture Credits

Alamy Stock Photo: Carlos Mora 29; J Ruscello 30 below left; JG Photography 13; ry3bee/Stockimo 30 above left.

Cristian Barnett/Octopus Publishing Group: 23, 51, 54, 64, 102, 159, 191.

Dreamstime: Lucy Brown 30 above right.

iStock: freedom_naruk/iStock 34–35.

James Hoffmann: 14, 43, 44, 56–59, 66, 86, 94b, 98, 106, 107, 110, 113, 124, 129, 134, 149, 155, 158, 182–89, 197, 217.

Shutterstock: Jess Kraft 26; Laura Vlieg 30 below right; Rachata Teyparsit 18.